Reflections

Also by Dr. Lewis

No Single Thread: Psychological Health in Family Systems
with W. Robert Beavers, John T. Gossett, and Virginia Austin Phillips

To Be A Therapist: The Teaching and Learning

How's Your Family?

Psychiatry in General Medical Practice
with Gene Usdin

The Family: Evaluation and Treatment
with Charles Hoffling

Treatment Planning in Psychiatry
with Gene Usdin

To Find A Way:
The Outcome of Hospital Treatment of Disturbed Adolescents
with John T. Gossett and F. David Barnhart

The Long Struggle: Well-Functioning, Working-Class Black Families
with John Looney

The Birth of the Family: An Empirical Inquiry

Swimming Upstream:
Teaching and Learning Psychotherapy in a Biological Era

The Monkey-Rope: A Psychotherapist's Reflections on Relationships

Marriage As A Search for Healing: Theory, Assessment, and Therapy

Disarming The Past: How an Intimate Relationship Can Heal Old Wounds
with John T. Gossett

Reflections on the Good Life:
A Psychotherapist Writes to His Grandchildren

Famous Marriages: What They Can Teach Us

Reflections

on Relationships with Self and Others

JERRY M. LEWIS, M.D.

ZEIG, TUCKER & THEISEN, INC.
Phoenix Arizona

Library of Congress Cataloging-in-Publication Data

Reflections : on relationships with self and others / Jerry M. Lewis, M.D.
p. cm.
Includes bibliographic references.
ISBN: 978-1-934442-32-6 (alk. Paper)
1. Psychotherapy 2. Intimacy (Psychology) 3. Family therapy
4. Marriage—Psychological aspects 5. Adult children of dysfunctional families I. Lewis, Jerry M. 1924 - II. Title.

Published by

Zeig, Tucker & Theisen, Inc.
3618 North 24th Street
Phoenix, AZ 85016

Manufactured in the United States of America

DEDICATION

For Pat with and for love over the past 60 years.
Let the music play on!

CONTENTS

Part II
On Relationships With Others

Part III
On Psychotherapy

PREFACE

Those clinicians who write do so for a variety of reasons. My experience is that writing serves as the primary purpose of clarifying and expanding what I know about a particular topic. There is also something inherently satisfying about believing that one better understands the diverse personalities, problems, and relationship patterns brought to me by those seeking my help. Writing about them seems to give them greater substance. It is as if one doesn't really know something well until one writes (or speaks) about it. From this perspective, writing is a dialogue with oneself.

When one publishes what one has written, a different dynamic comes into play. The clinical writer tries to influence how the reader thinks. The essays presented in this collection, all originally published in the *Psychiatric Times,* are my attempts to influence how readers think. They are meant, first of all, to transmit the excitement I experience about the continuing advances in our understanding of clinical topics. There is so much new information across such a wide variety of topics that it is difficult, perhaps really impossible, for one person to take it all in. My hope is that these clinical essays cover a broad enough range of new information that all clinician-readers will find one of more encourage new understanding. Whether it is the emerging studies of gene-environment interaction in various psychopathologies; the clinical utility of the concept of a narrative identity and its turning points; the intriguing studies of self-deception and its role in psychological health; the remarkable beginnings to the systematic study of internal object representations and their crucial role in development; the growing documentation of how the therapeutic alliance influences the outcome of psychotherapy; or others, the message is that there is much that is new and exciting going on in the mental health professions.

The reader may note that most of these clinical essays are constructed around either new research findings or my clinical experiences or, more likely, both. The interplay between clinical experiences and research needs emphasis because the psychotherapeutic professions often are accused of entrenched immunity to research findings. To whatever extent there is some validity to that charge, it needs corrective action. There is simply too much new resulting from contemporary research to not use it, and thus fail to offer our patients all that we might.

Another of my hopes is that these essays will stand against reductionism in our understanding of clinical phenomena. The accumulated evidence is overwhelming: All psychiatric disorders are multidetermined—there is no single etiologic factor that explains why a particular person develops a particular syndrome at a particular point in life. We need to understand, therefore, as many of the multiple factors involved in our patients' dilemmas as possible, and then consider the potential utility of different interventions based on that understanding.

The list of what I hope reading these essays may provoke in the reader's thinking about the clinical topics discussed could go on and on. To go beyond the impact on thinking, however, leads to feelings. I hope that the reader will experience something pleasurable, some sense of positive connection to this fellow clinician.

—Jerry M. Lewis, M.D., 2009
Dallas, Texas

ACKNOWLEDGEMENTS

There are many people to thank for the roles they have played in the writing of these clinical essays. At the top of my list are those who have taught me across the long span of my career as a therapist. Individual patients, couples, and families, of course, but also the hundreds of nonclinical subjects—research volunteers, applicants for the psychiatric residency program I directed for many years, and aspirants for the Episcopal priesthood and diaconate – have all instructed me.

Then there is a circle of close friends, psychiatrists and clinical psychologists, who have provided me with much – needed feedback. John Gossett and Carlos Davis, friends and colleagues at the Timberlawn Research Foundation continue to do so. Gene Usdin not only suggested to the Psychiatric Times that I become their clinical columnist but has been a major source of encouragement. As long as they were alive two other psychiatrists and close friends, Mike Zales and Harold Visotsky, did the same.

My wife, Part, and my grown children, two of whom are therapists themselves, have always been openly supportive of my writing and loving in their encouragement that I continue to have something useful to say.

I had been writing scientific articles and books for about 20 years when I began to experiment with brief clinical essays. When I showed some of them to my friend-publisher, Bernie Mazel, he graciously agreed to publish a collection of them. This resulted in The Monkey-Rope (Bernel Books, 1996, Lexington, Mass). Five years later I was approached by Christine Potvin, then editor of Psychiatric Times, to write the Practicing Column for that newspaper. I agreed and for the past seven years my bimonthly column has appeared. I am told that these essays are favorably received by the psychiatrists who read them, and they constitute this book.

I showed my columns to my friend and former editor at Brunner-Mazel, Suzi Tucker, who believed they could be published as a book. She sent them on to Jeff Zeig, her partner at Zeig, Tucker & Theisen, Inc. who agreed to publish them. Thus, I owe a debt of gratitude to Bernie, Christine, Suzi, and Jeff for implementing this book.

Finally, Velma Byford, my administrative assistant, has put each essay in written form and, as has been so for many years, I am in her debt.

INTRODUCTION

These clinical essays were originally published in the Practicing column of the *Psychiatric Times* and reflect my thinking on a broad range of clinical issues. They are the products of two deeply ingrained personal characteristics: I read and I write. My reading of the scientific literature is deeply ingrained and colleagues have often commented on its extensiveness. In part this reflects my age and the fact that I have lived through cycles of psychiatric ideologies in which one particular perspective has been dominant. During my training and early professional work psychoanalytic thinking was pervasive. Later social psychiatry with its central premise that here-and-now interpersonal relationships were crucial had its moment in the sun. For several decades neuroscientific advances and psychopharmacology have been most prominent. Each of these ideologies has influenced the way I think about clinical issues. I continue to sample their literatures—save for psychopharmacology which I find tedious and refer such issues to former residents who specialize in those matters. As will be reflected in several of the essays, I believe the most exciting new paradigm is that of the role of gene-environment interactions in producing psychopathology, a movement away from reductionism of earlier periods.

Reading more generally has been important to me for as long as I can remember. I was one of those kids who read under the covers with a flashlight in order to get around a bedtime, lights-out parental edict. Although more extraverted than introverted, I always had a book going. My reading was indiscriminate; I had no real guide to better literature, and it was only later as a young adult that I decided to begin to read the classics. For some years now I have read both contemporary fiction and nonfiction, but, curiously enough, only in the evenings. Daytime reading is always professional and my briefcase is usually stuffed with journal articles. The distinction between reading for pleasure and reading for work, however, is not useful for me: both are pleasurable. What may be idiosyncratic, perhaps neurotic, about my reading is that although I can read for work in the evenings, I cannot read for pleasure (fiction, etc.) during the daytime hours. It just doesn't feel right. There is probably some unconscious connection between this rule (no reading solely for pleasure during the day) and my childhood struggle with my parents' rules about lights-out but the details of that connection continue to elude me.

Writing came later. I did not do so as a child or adolescent. My first piece of serious writing grew out of a medical student research project involving the hemodynamics of congestive heart failure. Later during a research fellowship in psychiatry I helped write an article on teaching guinea pigs how to have asthma. These early ventures in writing for professional audiences—particularly since they involved systematically collected research data—excited me. When I finished my training and returned to Dallas to join the then small staff at Timberlawn Psychiatric Hospital, I searched for ways to continue writing. One opportunity was to involve the residents in clinical research and publish the results and another was to write clinical articles for nonpsychiatric physicians. All of this changed some years later when I became the director of the Timberlawn Psychiatric Research Foundation and began programs of clinical research (treatment outcome studies, family system research, and other topics). These research projects produced publishable articles and books. My career then came to involve 20 hours per week in each of three domains; hospital leadership positions, clinical research, and psychotherapy. The diversity suited me well, and each domain brought satisfactions. The need, however, to continue writing persisted. I believe I am aware of some of its roots. Most of all my writing is an act of self-clarification. The need to clarify what I think I know about a topic is powerfully augmented by putting my thoughts on paper. As a consequence, much of what I write is not intended for publication; rather it is part of my dialogue with myself.

Another reason for my writing is that like reading I find writing pleasurable. At its most simple level using pencils (only Murado Black Warriors) and yellow legal-sized paper must activate those circuits in my brain that result in something like endorphin production. I do not know why this is so for me—it just is.

A third reason involves those pieces that I decide to publish. It is a way of connecting to others, and when something I have written leads to letters, emails, or phone calls from other professionals there is a deep sense of satisfaction (only the laudatory seem to communicate).

About 15 years ago I began to write essays on clinical topics. I liked in particular that these mostly 1200-1500 word essays, in contrast to my other writing, were easy to finish. Each essay took four to six hours to write (and rewrite) and then there was a sense of completion. Much of my professional life has centered about psychotherapy and research. These gratifying experiences almost always involved many months, even years of effort and did not satisfy my need for completion. I experienced the same sense of completion on my tractor when, before both my wife and my internist called a halt, I could cut the three or four acres around our lakehouse. As I finished and looked back at the freshly cut field, there was a deep sense of pleasurable completion. I am uncertain about the roots of pleasurable completion, but think it may be present in many persons, particularly those of us with some compulsive traits. At any rate, writing these clinical essays brings me the same sense of pleasurable completion as my tractor work formerly did.

Another factor involved in writing these brief clinical essays is that doing so allows me to range broadly across many topics. I have just completed, for example, a short book on the psychology of religious callings. This book grew out of my role in evaluating the psychological status of aspirants for the Episcopal priesthood and diaconate. I inquired about calling experiences, thought I heard several different themes in their narratives, and found nothing in the psychological literature about callings. The book resulted, and though I hope it offers a first look at an often life-changing experience, it is a narrow topic. These essays—in their very number—allow me to range across many topics. I finished my residency over 50 years ago and continue to practice as an individual and marital-family therapist at age 84. I believe these years have involved bumping up against many of the major issues confronting the disciplines of psychiatry, psychology, and psychiatric social work. Further, as noted earlier, I read a lot of scientific literature. Several years ago, for example, and for reasons of space I weeded out over 6000 of collected reprints, cutting them to an irreducible 150. The point is that as a result of a long practice of the psychotherapies and my reading habits I find topics for these essays come relatively easy to mind.

Although I find pleasurable both the reading and the writing that go into these clinical essays, I also hope that readers find them useful. Most of all the writer part of me hopes that other clinicians will be encouraged by their reading of them to rethink some of the ways they have thought about these clinical topics. That is the ultimate goal of their publication together—not to persuade but to provoke.

Part I

On Relationship With Oneself

1

HOW MANY SELVES DOES A PERSON HAVE?

After a good deal of reading and thinking about the evolution and current status of the self, I asked my wife of 55 years how many selves she had. She smiled and said, "Four. There's my private self, my self with you, myself with our children and grandchildren, and myself with close friends." I responded, "How much of your private self is apparent in our relationship?" She smiled again and said, "Probably 75 percent." "Damn", I said, "We've been married 55 years and you're still 25 percent a stranger." She laughed and told me that was about right.

There are several issues involved in this interchange. The first is that my wife said she had four selves, one private and three oriented to the roles of wife, mother-grandmother, and close friend. More about this later. The second involves that she also said that 75 percent of her private self was apparent in our relationship—25 percent of her private self remained hidden. It is this issue that I wish to address first.

How much can one know about what goes on inside another person? Is 75 percent high or low? What remains undisclosed, even in an intense, long-lasting relationship? First, a bit about the context of our relationship. The 55 years of our being together (58 if you include the three years of courtship as student nurse and medical student) have been remarkably harmonious. No chronic conflict despite very different personalities. A good deal of psychological intimacy as in the exchange of vulnerabilities. No serious individual emotional disturbances. No truly distressing problems in raising four children who have turned out to be caring, successful adults. Further, we talk about psychological issues often, read the same novels, and, for the most part, like the same people. With the exception of my writing and her tennis we enjoy the same activities. In light of all these positives, is 75 percent high or low? I don't know the answer. There are, as far as I know, no reported systematic data.

As I think about this issue of how much one can know another, a long-ago conversation with a good friend comes to mind. He was in the later stages of his training analysis, and, for reasons I can't recall, our talk turned to how completely he disclosed himself to his training analyst. Two things stand out. First, he said he knew of his analyst's theoretical interests and skewed his reflections and associations in those directions. In other words, he was sensitive to his analyst's mind set—what might please him—even at the cost of disregarding the injunction to say whatever came to mind. The need to please important others is a major influence on that which we disclose. Second, he reported that there were several issues he avoided in order to finish the analysis. The lesson here is that pragmatic goals are also an important determinant of how much and what one discloses to an important other.

The issue is a fascinating one, and I shall continue to think about it, but wish to turn now to the fact that my wife said, without hesitation, that she had four selves. Does a person have one self or multiple selves? The literature in this regard is unclear. For the most part, students of the self have traditionally endorsed the idea of a singular self as a marker of psychological health. If the self is defined as experienced identity (rather than as total psychology of a person), there is growing emphasis on the narrative structure of the self. This view holds that the self is experienced as an evolving autobiographical narrative that, when successful, provides the person with the sense that his or her life has coherence. Without coherence it is difficult to find meaning in one's life, and the existentialists tell us that finding meaning is an ultimate concern.

McAdams has been in the forefront of those writing about the narrative self and bases much of his perspective on his own research and that of others (1). The self-narrative has a distinctive tone (e.g.

optimism), a particular imagery (e.g. dramatic with often unexpected events), emphasizes the broad themes of power (e.g. competence, strength, impact) and intimacy (e.g. relationships, caring), contains one or several turning points, includes an ideological base (e.g. religious, ethical), and involves several, sometimes conflicting, portrayals of the self.

McAdams has reported on the nature of self-narrative of highly generative adults, the longitudinal impact of high intimacy motivation on marital stability, the roles of both redemptive (turning bad situations to good) and contaminating (turning good situations to bad) narrative strategies on midlife generativity, and other intriguing research findings.

The characteristics of a self-narrative are in the service of maintaining a sense of coherence to one's identity. As such, the self-narrative can be understood as an integrating process that enables a person to believe that he or she remains essentially the same despite the so-often confusing primal stew of life experience.

There is, however, considerable evidence that narrative coherence is purchased by the use of usually benign illusions. The past is reconstructed (usually negatively) in order to buttress the belief that one has progressed or matured. The present is experienced in often unrealistic terms (most persons report being "above average" on a broad variety of personal characteristics). The future is seen as more positive and under greater control than base rate data justify. These illusions—if not extreme—are believed to be adaptive in that they help maintain the coherence of the single self.

The singular self as a marker of psychological health has been challenged recently by those who posit that a person has several (or many) selves, and that health is the ability to sustain multiple versions of the self. Mitchell writes, for example, about the changing psychoanalytic perspective (2). The idea of a singular, integrated self is being replaced by the view of multiple selves emerging in different contexts for different purposes. Knowing only one version of oneself is often a defense against knowing and being distressed by other versions of the self. Ackerman, in writing about the brain's alchemy, suggests that the brain is a gifted illusionist in that it has the capacity to render the many selves that accompany us everywhere into a fluent, stable sense of self (3). She also notes that we have no idea where to pinpoint the sense of self in the brain despite the remarkable advances in imaging techniques. The light may be seen on the porch, she writes, without telling us who is inside the house.

Mitchell and Ackerman are but examples of those who write about multiple selves, and despite their persuasiveness, it seems to me that the issue of singular self versus multiple selves is far from settled. Those who support the construct of a singular self often write about the ability to recognize and sustain internal contradictions. The capacity to recognize that one is both good and evil, powerful and helpless, altruistic and selfish, and other basic human contradictions and to incorporate these insights in a single integrated sense of self is a marker of the mature adult. In other words, the presence of much that is contradictory within the self does not require the conclusion of multiple selves. Having multiple selves, as in multiple personality disorder, is a pathological outcome centrally involving the failure to sustain and integrate basic human contradictions.

In truth, I don't know what to make of the idea that a person has multiple selves. I have spent too many years as a therapist with the idea that maturity is reflected in a single self able to integrate internal contradictions that it may be my reluctance to give up a familiar model. In some ultimate way the issue may be utility. Is it more useful for a therapist to believe that the self is plural? If so, how? What would change about therapeutic interventions? I can't find ready answers to these and other questions. And, yet, my wife, not familiar with the theory of the self, said, "Four." Very interesting.

References

1. McAdams, D.P. (1993). *The Stories We Live By: Personal Myths and the Making of the Self.* New York: The Guilford Press.
2. Mitchell, S.A. (2002). *Can Love Last?* New York: W.W. Norton & Co.
3. Ackerman, D. (2004). *An Alchemy of Mind.* New York: Scribners.

November 2004

2

INTERNAL CONTRADICTIONS AND DOUBT

I saw him for many years, and his changing symptoms were a disservice to descriptive diagnostic systems and ideas of clearly bounded brain diseases. Over the 25 years of our doctor-patient relationship he fulfilled at different times the diagnostic criteria for major depression, bipolar disorder, paranoid schizophrenia, and, when not psychotic, was profoundly obsessional. His pervasive obsessional thinking led to paralyzing doubt. He literally doubted everything about himself: whether he was who he was suppose to be; whether his parents and siblings were really his relatives; whether he had gone to college for several years before his problems overwhelmed him; whether he was taking in enough fluids; whether his chronically schizophrenic sister was playacting; the list goes on and on.

Contrast this patient's pervasive and crippling doubt with the absence of doubt encountered in the father of a family I saw briefly in family therapy. This man expressed absolute certainty about everything, and his level of conviction was an almost insurmountable impediment to conversation. He did not talk with others; rather, he made pronouncements. When I tried in family therapy to introduce the idea that in relationships subjective reality was usually more important than truth, his fury filled the room. He seemed totally incapable of doubt.

Although most of us fall somewhere between these two extremes, it may be useful to consider what our current understanding is of the meanings of doubt during adult life. First, it is important to know that two of the most influential investigators of adult ego development, George Vaillant and Jane Loevinger, present data concerning this issue (1) (2). Their agreement that the ability to sustain paradox (with resulting doubt) is one of the markers of ego maturity is remarkable in that they have used widely different methods of studying ego development. Vaillant has used a variety of methods, including a primary emphasis on intensive interviewing, to study three samples of subjects who have been followed for over fifty years. Loevinger has developed a widely used sentence completion test that, for the most part, has been used to study a huge number of persons of different ages and backgrounds.

The ability to sustain paradox is considered one part of the development of complex thinking during the adult years. Although complex thinking has many components, the ability to think about one's own thoughts is a basic feature. Both Vaillant and Loevinger rely on the studies of cognitive development, particularly those of Piaget, as one important aspect of ego development (3).

In my view, the capacity to sustain doubt evolves out of the ability to be in touch with one's own internal paradoxes or contradictions. This perspective rests on the belief that an essential part of the human condition involves the presence of inevitable contradictory needs, wishes, drives, affects, ego states, or basic conflicts. This belief is as old as recorded history and underlies much of contemporary psychological theory. In offering the following six fundamental internal contradictions, my debt to Levinson's work is acknowledged (4). These six contradictions are not meant to be inclusive, but are those heard most often from both my patients and research volunteer subjects.

1. Separateness - Connectedness. This contradiction involves the realization that one is both alone and intimately involved with others. It deals with the extent that one's experience of oneself is at different times that of being separate, independent, and autonomous and at other times of being part of a system of relationships. I am both a "me" and a "we."
2. Love and Hate. This contradiction, often called ambivalence, is the realization that, try as hard as we may, inevitably we hurt those we love.

3. Good and Evil. This involves the understanding that one has the capacity to do good, to be altruistic and, at other times, to act in ways that our self-interests prevail at the expense of the welfare of others.
4. Powerful and Helpless. This realization involves the experience that one is strong, impactful, and in charge of one's destiny and the contradictory realization that life is altered by circumstances over which one has no control.
5. Old and Young. During adult years there is the contradiction between believing that life is more or less unending and the realization that the body decays and death awaits.
6. Masculine and Feminine. The contradiction lies between the belief that one is entirely masculine or feminine and the understanding that one's self contains ingredients of what the culture defines as both masculine and feminine.

These contradictions can be understood as the ongoing adult outcomes of life-long developmental processes involving attachment, narcissism, aggression, morality, and sexual identity. The ability to be in touch with them is a marker of mature cognitive development. Their recognition and the ability to sustain them are important aspects of one's relationship to oneself and are considered markers of ego maturity.

I select the verb "sustain" rather than "resolve" to describe what I believe to be an optimal outcome. Sustaining means living with, and, under the best circumstances, may lead to the ability to respond empathically to the dilemmas of others. Resolution involves the risk of absolutism, the conviction that there is but one way and those who do not subscribe are inferior, doomed, or dangerous.

The first patient described had not developed or had lost the capacity to face his internal contradictions. As a consequence his life was chaotic; doubts invaded every aspect of his experience of self. Although before he experienced symptoms he had made friends and finished two years of college, his illness developed in the context of his first attempts at a heterosexual relationship. Whether it was this experience—involving the need to face the internal contradictions of separateness-connectedness, love-hate, powerful-helpless, and masculine-feminine—that led to his retreat from life is but one way to frame his haunting dilemma.

The father in the family therapy vignette also could not sustain his internal contradictions. One or more of them can be understood as provoking such intense anxiety that all paradox had to be banished from his consciousness. The result was an escape from a feared chaos to a very limited or circumscribed self. His resulting rigid, linear thinking may have saved him from a worse outcome, but had malignant impact on his family.

As I look back at my own experiences, the religiosity of my adolescence and the scientism of my young adulthood can be understood as attempts to resolve doubt—to believe that either faith or proof can lead to the absence of uncertainty. Now and for many years I have been more intrigued than anything else on those occasions when my thoughts, feelings, fantasies, dreams, or feedback from important others puts me in touch with internal contradictions. I wonder how this change evolved. How much of it results from an empathic wife, my work as a therapist, the maturation of my brain, or who knows what other factors? What I do think I know is that doubt, at least at certain levels, can be a comfortable companion. Further, I suggest that the ability to be in touch with one's internal contradictions and to sustain them—to tolerate doubt—is an important attribute of the effective psychotherapist.

References

1. Vaillant, G.E. (1993). *The Wisdom of The Ego.* Cambridge, MA: Harvard University Press.
2. Loevinger, J. (1976). *Ego Development.* San Francisco: Jossey-Bass.
3. Piaget, J. (1970). "Piaget's Theory" in *Carmichael's Manual of Child Psychology,* P.H. Mussen (Ed). New York: John Wiley & Sons.
4. Levinson, D.J. (1978). *The Season's of a Man's Life.* New York: Ballantine Books.

March 2002

3

HOW MUCH SELF-DECEPTION HELPS?

He came to see me because his wife, in psychoanalytic psychotherapy with a colleague, had insisted that he change his anger, remoteness, and controllingness if she was to stay in the relationship. He described an emotionally deprived childhood, an isolated adolescence, and an early adulthood devoted to achieving economic success. His sense of his present self differed markedly, however, from his wife's assessment. "I really used to be very troubled," he reported, "but years of therapy changed all of that. Now I believe I am healthy; the problem is my wife's insatiable needs." His current positive self-assessment, however, was at least partially contradicted by his lack of eye contact, flat affect, and rigid posture.

Although this clinical vignette contains many possible dynamic interpretations, it is used here to introduce the issue of the role of self-deception in both psychological adaptation and psychopathology. Is, for example, some degree of self-deception adaptive? At what level does self-deception become maladaptive? Can self-deception be adaptive for the individual and toxic to his or her important relationships?

There is a surprising amount of systematic research probing various aspects of self-deception. One stream of research involves distorting the past to better accommodate the present. Narrative approaches to individual identity emphasize the continuing unconscious altering of the recollected past in order to feel better about the present. Such distorted memories often involve recalling earlier circumstances as worse than they may have been. When faced with clear evidence of their distortions of that past, some subjects react with much anxiety, and it has been suggested that the anxiety stems from the interruption of the sense of a coherent life story identity.

Most adults, excepting the elderly, have been demonstrated to derogate their past psychological status and see themselves as having undergone considerable positive change during adulthood. Three factors may play roles in such self-perceptions. One is that longitudinal adult developmental research suggests that many adults continue to mature. "I am much more stable than I was earlier" may be accurate reporting. The second explanation is that persons reporting much improvement during adult years are responding to a pervasive cultural mandate that values progress. People are supposed to mature, grow, and make progress in life. The third factor is that of self-deception. The exaggeration of past woes is in the service of feeling better about one's current self. Although all three factors may operate to varying degrees in different persons, recent longitudinal research speaks to the ubiquity of some degree of self-deception in many persons. Offer and his colleagues, for example, studied adolescents at age 14 and again when the subjects were 48 (1). There was no statistically significant correlation between their answers to the same questions at 14 and 48. Selected examples include that at age 14, 11 percent of the subjects reported negatively about the emotional climate of the home, but 50 percent did so at age 48. During the 34 year interval the percentage reporting family conflict increased from 13 percent to 33 percent. Although there was considerable variation from topic to topic, the trend was to recollect more negatively at 48 than reported at 14.

Studies like this inevitably bring to mind personal experiences. One such involved finding a large bundle of letters I had written to my mother while in the service during World War II. The picture they paint of life in my early family is much more positive than I recall thinking then or have thought since. Another personal experience is my wife's observation that I began to describe my early family environment much more negatively after I changed from internal medicine to a psychiatric residency. It is hard to sort out all the factors at play. Separation from family during wartime, new insights gained during my psychiatric training, a new set of family experiences with my wife and young children, and others are all possible. Have I been deceiving myself by derogating my past experiences and functioning in order to feel good about my current self? Like most others, my life story identity resists corrections of fact, but self-deception cannot be ruled out.

Another large stream of research involves the concept of adaptive illusions. Here the focus is not on the past but on the present and future. Janoff-Bulman, for example, presents research findings from the study of severe life trauma that support the presence of three adaptive illusions that are shattered by randomness (2). They are:

1. One's own world (rather than the world at large) is benevolent, people are basically good, and, as a consequence, one is safe; 2. The world is meaningful in the sense that misfortune is not random, people by and large get what they deserve, justice prevails, and persons are consequently in control of their own outcomes; 3. One is worthy and deserving of the best (almost everyone reports being better than average across a wide range of personality characteristics!). These illusions of safety, control, and self-worth are overgeneralizations that both allow one to live more comfortably in an often random world and need at least partial repair when randomness strikes.

Other studies demonstrate that most people describe themselves in unrealistically positive terms, believe they have greater control in life than is possible, and anticipate the future more positively than base-rate data justify (3). Further, such adaptive illusions are associated with standard measures of mental health. Thus, the research suggests that, within limits, some degree of self-deception contributes to mental health. The adage "know thyself" as an unfettered road to mental health appears to require at least one minor qualification.

The patient described in the opening vignette presented a relatively straight forward clinical situation. He proved to have more self-deception than described in the literature on adaptive illusions, and a lengthy treatment was required to help him relax his denial. My sense was that this individual work was necessary, and that a couples therapy format would have been ineffective, perhaps disastrous, until he was better able to sort out his wife's accurate confrontations from her projections.

The research on self-deception in nonclinical populations, however, does have clinical implications. It speaks most of all to how important it is to feel good about oneself in the here-and-now and how we may unknowingly derogate somewhat our past selves, exaggerate current positive characteristics, and view the future through rose-tinted glasses in the service of maintaining current self-esteem. The fact that there are data indicating that such mild self-deceptions are not pathological but associated with other indices of mental health needs emphasis lest some sort of self-deception syndrome is included in our next diagnostic manual.

References

1. Offer, D., Kaiz, M., Howard, K.I., Bennett, E.S. (2000). "The Altering of Reported Experiences." J Am Acad Child Adolesc Psychiatry, June, 39:6, 735-742.
2. Janoff-Bulman, R. (1992). *Shattered Assumptions: Toward a New Psychology of Trauma*. New York: The Free Press.
3. Taylor, S.E., Brown, J.D. (1988). "Illusion and Well-Being: A Social Psychological Perspective on Mental Health." Psychological Bulletin, 103, 195-210.

July 2004

4

RECONSTRUCTING ONE'S PAST

Over 55 years ago I graduated from the then almost new medical school in Dallas and went off to Boston and the Brigham to be a straight medical intern. Married for two years and with my wife pregnant with our first child, I and we knew not a soul in Boston. I was on duty for 36 of each 48 hours (excepting one weekend a month) and of little help to my wife who was alone in a strange city and facing the imminent birth of our first child. It was, in short, not an easy year. However, we made friends and I was encouraged to stay on at the Brigham. We not only survived but, in a sense, flourished. Although from a developmental perspective, survival and growth are important markers of outcome, there is more to the ways in which those experiences changed us than those markers suggest.

One change concerned what was to become my career in psychiatry. In the Dallas of the early 50s psychiatry was overwhelming biologic. There were no helpful psychotropic drugs, and the prevalent treatment paradigms involved electroshock, insulin coma, and, for some, sleep therapy. In Boston psychoanalysis was the clearly dominant ideology, and whether stated explicitly or accepted implicitly it was based in part on the biblical injunction that knowing the truth shall set you free. As a psychoanalytic premise, however, the biblical injunction was understood as knowing the truth about oneself led to freedom from maladaptive behavioral patterns learned in childhood. This emphasis on truth and the search for insight attracted some of the very brightest of my fellow house officers in Boston, and had a major impact on my evolving ideas about human psychology.

How much things have changed since those early days! My reading of the current understanding of what one discovers about oneself in many forms of psychotherapy is not necessarily the truth but rather a more useful reconceptualization of one's personal past. The emphasis on truth has been replaced by that of utility. What, it is now asked, is the most helpful way of understanding one's personal past?

This movement away from the search for truth as a guiding principle of many psychotherapeutic schools has been influenced during the past 50 years by multiple factors. In this essay I will discuss only three; longitudinal studies, narrative theory, and neuroscientific advances, particularly regarding memory.

Longitudinal studies suggest that many adults' recollections of their pasts—especially childhood and family experiences—undergo changes throughout life. One "truth" is replaced by another. For some the parents of childhood, for example, are recalled more sympathetically. For others the recollections are much more critical. Some believe that the difference between those who are more sympathetic and those who are more critical is to be found in the present circumstances of those doing the recollecting. We found support for this premise in a longitudinal study of young couples before and after the birth of their first child (1, 2). In the findings relevant to this topic, the research subjects' reports of their childhood relationships with each parent and the nature of their parents' marriage were relatively stable from the prenatal period to four years after the birth of their first child. Having a child and parenting that child for four years did not appear to induce systematic changes in the recollections of their own childhoods. There was, however, one intriguing exception to this picture of relative continuity. A number of the women subjects changed their recollections of their fathers from positive to negative. After four years of parenting they no longer recalled their fathers as affectionate and supportive during their childhoods as they had prior to the birth of their child. In searching to understand the correlates of these changed memories we found a clear pattern, and it had to do not with the women subjects but their husbands. The women who changed their recollections had husbands who were depressed, helped little with parenting, and were observed to be less sensitive to their children than other fathers were. Why, then, would the women with less available and helpful husbands change their recollections of their fathers in a negative way? One possible answer to this question was found in the marital satisfaction data. The women with depressed, unhelpful husbands did not report lower levels of marital satisfaction; rather they were maintained at high levels. One interpretation of our data was that the women's more negative memories of their fathers served the function of minimizing (or denying) their husbands' failures to be as helpful as needed. If this is all that can be expected of men I can no longer recall my father so positively.

Although there are other interpretations of these data, the central issue is that they demonstrate that reconstructions of the past may be in the service of adapting to present circumstances.

The second factor impacting on the diminished emphasis on the truth is the growth of narrative theory and its extension into the study of the self. There is a vast literature on these topics, and, for reasons of space, I will refer only to the work of McAdams whose theoretical writing and empirical research on the narrative self has been particularly illuminating for me (see, for example, 3). McAdams suggests that personality can be conceptualized as a three level entity. Personality traits occupy one level and these partially inherited characteristics are relatively unchanging during adult life. The second level, personal concerns, includes a wide array of important characteristics (e.g. values, defense mechanisms, etc.) that often change during adult development. The third level is the autobiographical self, the story one tells oneself and important others about one's life—its past, present, and anticipated future. This narrative is believed to undergo subtle but constant revision usually outside the person's awareness. Indeed, if confronted with clear evidence of revisions, most persons become distressed.

The major revisionary process is altering the memories of the past to better fit the present. Many students of the narrative self believe that these reconstructions are in the service of coherence. In order to maintain a coherent sense of self in an often unpredictable world, one modifies the past. Here, again, as in the longitudinal study reviewed above, it is the present that changes the past.

The third influence on the lessened emphasis on the truth are the views of some memory researchers. Gilbert reviews this research and describes the picture that comes together of how memory actually works (4). We are unable to store all that we experience over time - there is simply too much to handle even for our complex brains. Rather, experiences are compressed for storage by being reduced to a few key elements. When we want to recall a particular experience "our brains quickly reweave the tapestry by fabricating—not by actually retrieving—the bulk of the information that we experience as a memory" (4, p. 87). All of this happens so quickly that we believe it was all in our heads all the time.

The laboratory research that documents this process is voluminous and establishes the fact that information obtained after an event may alter the memory of the event. (Here, again, the impact of present on past). Gilbert suggests that most scientists have become convinced that remembering involves "filling in" details that were not actually stored and this process occurs outside of the awareness of the remembering person.

In this essay I have suggested some of the factors that have altered the romantic paradigm of my early psychiatric experiences—that the truth can set one free. In its place has crept the paradigm of utility. The objective of some forms of psychotherapy is to assist patients in rewriting their narrative selves into a form that provides both greater understanding and relief from pain. Almost immediately, however, it is important to point out that not just any revision of the patient's life narrative will do. The revision must include all that is "known" to have happened to the patient, should emphasize the importance of the patient's decisions on his or her life course, and should represent a collaborative process shared by patient and therapist.

I suspect that some reading will disagree with my formulation of these changes, and, in truth, I hope so. Such would reassure that these issues are still alive in a field that often seems dominated by diagnoses and prescriptions.

References

1. Lewis, J.M., Owen, M.T., & Cox, M.J. (1989). "Family of Origin" (pp. 89-99) in J.M. Lewis, the *Birth of the Family: An Empirical Inquiry*. New York: Brunner-Mazel.
2. Lewis, J.M. & Owen, M.T. (1995). "Stability and Change in Family-of-Origin Recollections Over the First Four Years of Parenthood." Family Process, 34: 455-469.
3. McAdams, D.P. (1996). *Power, Intimacy, and the Life Story: Personological Inquiries Into Identity,* New York: The Guildford Press.
4. Gilbert, Daniel. (2007). *Stumbling on Happiness.* New York: Vintage Books.

August 2008

5

THE REHABILITATION OF ONENESS

He was young, schizoid, and had experienced brief periods of psychotic-like disorganization. We worked together in psychotherapy for many years. None of the then-available psychotropic agents was helpful. He believed, however, that marijuana was helpful, and, if he had smoked a joint in the hours preceding a session, his way of relating to me was different. He was less "there," more deeply into himself. His descriptions of the marijuana experience never varied. "I am," he would say, "at peace. I feel connected to everything. I am part of the universe, part of nature, part of God." He was, I thought, a person with significant ego boundary problems who, for the most part, maintained his basic sense of self by distancing himself from both the world and inner turmoil. Marijuana appeared to lead to the internal experience of greater connectedness and peace, although I felt he was less available to me after using it.

Does this young man's experience of peaceful merger have any relationship to spiritual or mystical experiences, often thought of as self-transcendence, in which what is described also centrally involves merger (usually with God or nature) and great inner peace? I have heard such experiences described by some of the candidates I have evaluated for the Episcopal priesthood, but these persons showed no evidence of schizoid or other major psychopathology. This observation that experiences of merger appear to occur in persons with very different personalities and in very different contexts has attracted the interest of academics from multiple disciplines for many years. Psychiatry, however, has until perhaps quite recently, only pathologized merger experiences.

Fifty years ago any suggestion of a person's merger with the surround was seen in psychiatry as clearly pathological. As a resident I was taught that such experiences strongly suggested an underlying psychotic process. In retrospect it is hard not to conclude that the then-prominent psychoanalytic emphasis on separation-individuation as the major (or only) process underlying healthy development may have played a role in pathologizing oneness experiences that appear to be the opposite of sharp self-object distinctions.

As they say, a lot has happened on the way to the forum. During the last 50 years psychoanalytic thinking has become much more relational. Healthy development is now seen as the product of both separation-individuation and the processes underlying the capacity for psychological intimacy. Intimacy is defined as shared subjectivity, a temporary merger of sorts. This increased theoretical emphasis on relational processes has had many implications. One of these has been a more process-oriented understanding of ego boundaries.

Polster, for example, has written of the need to rework the old physicalistic conception of ego boundaries with its emphasis on delineating the person from his or her surround to a more dynamic, process-oriented set of functions that, under the best of circumstances, allow moment-by-moment oscillation between separateness and inclusion (1). As such, ego boundaries are more accurately understood as describing the ongoing relationship between person and surround rather than as solely characteristics of the person. Polster suggests, however, that each person has a characteristic balance of the processes of inclusion and separateness. For purposes of this essay, however, what needs emphasis is that she suggests that the continuum of inclusion includes at one, not necessarily pathologic extreme, "oceanic feelings of oneness, union, or merger with the surround" (p. 257).

Not necessarily pathologic does not, however, imply that experiences of oneness can be good for the person. Good here is used in the sense of psychological growth. The premise that oneness experiences may have positive impact takes us back to the controversial work of Silverman, the subliminal presentation of the "Mommy and I are one" stimulus, and the subsequent temporary improvement across a wide variety of psychological functions. Silverman, a psychologist-psychoanalyst, was interested in lab experiments testing the validity of psychoanalytic concepts and published scores of studies for almost 30 years (see, for example, 2). His early interest was in the role of unconscious symbiotic fantasies in schizophrenia. He and his associates presented the sentence, "Mommy and I are one" tachistoscopically at speeds that were unreadable. In the short term many schizophrenic subjects showed improved functioning in several psychological processes (e.g., fewer cognitive distortions) that was not shown following similar presentations of nonsymbiotic material.

To make a long and complex story manageable in this essay, Silverman prompted a major uproar in academic circles. As his work was extended to persons without schizophrenia and the same positive impact shown, the disbelief grew. As investigators not associated with Silverman verified many of his findings, the uproar continued. I have known, for example, several serious thinkers in psychology who can only discuss Silverman's work with clear contempt. I have wondered whether this reflects Silverman's early conclusion that there exists in all persons an unconscious wish for reunion with the early good mother.

In 1990 Hardaway published a quantitative review and metanalysis of 56 studies involving 111 different samples (3). He concluded that, despite the need for various methodologic improvements, there is a clear and robust conclusion that the subliminal activation of symbiotic fantasies ("Mommy and I are one") increased temporary adaptability across a wide variety of subjects with various preconditions and tested in a number of labs. It is impossible to read this careful overview and not to conclude that there is something to the oneness construct, whether symbiotic or not. Psychology and psychiatry need to attend more closely to the theoretical and clinical relevance of experiences or merger, oneness, and self-transcendence.

Support for this position has recently surfaced from an improbable source—the use of brain scan technology to study mystical states. Once again, for reasons of space, I will refer only to one source of this work. d'Aquili and Newberg have presented findings that suggest during periods of loss of self-world distinctions in meditation and intense prayer similar portions of the brain are activated (or deactivated) (4). Although this intriguing work is with small numbers of subjects and the experimental methods are complex, the findings are provocative. For present purposes, however, I note that these investigators have suggested a continuum of unitary experiences. Starting with "baseline reality" the continuum moves to aesthetic experiences (sunsets and symphonies) to romantic love. Next come numinous experiences (spiritual-religious), cosmic consciousness, progressive trance states, and the continuum ends with experiences of "absolute unity" which includes the obliteration of time and space. Although one can easily question the ordering of this continuum of oneness, it does encourage a thoughtful re-examination of oneness phenomena in our understanding of the self and its pathologies.

It seems to me that oneness is gradually undergoing a type of rehabilitation. Exactly where this will lead and what implications it may have for clinical work are impossible to know at the present time. Perhaps the important message for clinicians is to say open to future possibilities rather than holding on to earlier theory-based assumptions.

References

1. Polster, S. (1983). "Ego Boundary as Process: A systemic-Contextual Approach." Psychiatry, 46:247-258, August.
2. Silverman, L.H., Lachmann, F.M., and Melich, R.H. (1982). *The Search for Oneness*. Madison, CT: International Universities Press.
3. Hardaway, R.A. (1990). "Subliminally Activated Symbiotic Fantasies: Facts and Artifacts." Psychological Bulletin. Vol. 107, No. 2, 177-195.
4. d'Aquili, E., Newberg, A.B. (1999). *The Mystical Mind: Probing the Biology of Religious Experiences.* Minneapolis, MN: Fortress Press.

June 2007

6

ADULT GROWTH, INTERNALIZATIONS AND SYNAPTOGENESIS

Clinicians, I believe, have little opportunity to learn about adult psychological growth other than that which results from psychotherapy. Almost by definition, those who come for psychotherapy have not experienced major periods of growth arising out of other life experiences. A different picture emerges when one has the opportunity to interview in depth nonclinical subjects. Here the subjects' life narratives often contain major turning points that appear to usher in periods of psychological growth. During many decades I have had the opportunity to interview—usually in depth—over 800 nonclinical subjects. Research volunteers, applicants for a psychiatric residency, and, more recently, candidates for ordination in the Episcopal ministry came for interviews as one part of what was required to attain other goals. Some, certainly far from all, of these subjects described major life turning points.

> A 33 year-old physician applying for a psychiatric residency after several years of practice as a radiologist described her earlier self as intense, driven, and uncomfortable with emotional closeness. The turning point in her life involved her relationship with her new husband. "There is a calmness about Jim," she said, "an ability to enjoy the moment, an acceptance of life's uncertainty, and a deep empathy with others. Somehow—first with him and now more generally—I began to be less tense and

driven. Most of all, I'm less rigidly structured—more able to just hang loose. He's the best thing that ever happened to me."

He was 47, married with two teenage daughters, and practicing law part-time as he attended a local seminary. His law practice had been successful and, he said, enjoyable. Always religious and for years a leader in his parish church, he had no thoughts of the priesthood until, eight years earlier, he developed a major depression. The combination of an antidepressant and psychotherapy had been very helpful, and, as he gradually recovered, he found himself spending more and more time thinking about his life's meaning. "It was," he said, "as if I began to recognize that my life had been totally centered on career, marriage, and family—that it was, in a strange way, very self-oriented. I spent a lot of time talking with my wife about it, and she encouraged me to continue to explore other options. I began also to meet with my priest and, after a year or so he raised the question of whether God was calling me to the priesthood. More and more I came to feel that way—that I could serve Him through helping others. The whole process has changed who I am: I've found an inner peace I've never felt before."

She was 42 and described herself as a survivor. "All my life, she said, "I've had to deal with unusual stress. First, I was an only child, and my parents were killed in an accident when I was 11. I lived with my grandparents until I was 17 and went off to college. Had to pay for it myself—my grandparents couldn't—so I worked several jobs while I took classes. After graduation I got a good job and was successful. Many promotions and all of that. When I was 32 I met my husband, and we were very happy. Four years ago he developed a brain tumor and was dead in three months. I was absolutely devastated but kept working. Relied some on my friends but mostly I struggled on my own. One day at a time. Finally, I got into therapy—which was very hard for me to do because except for my husband, I've always kept my personal feelings to myself. But my therapist was wonderful—she very gradually got me more in touch with my hurt and rage about important others abandoning me. She also helped me become less distant and defensive—more open with others. My several years of therapy really changed who I am—or, at the least, who I feel myself to be.

These three much abbreviated vignettes illustrate several of the most commonly heard turning points in the life narratives of nonclinical subjects. Healing marriages, religious—spiritual experiences, and psychotherapy all involve a new and transforming relationship with either another person or with God. Each of the new relationships is described as leading to changes in the self—changes that sound like manifestations of psychological growth. Some readers may react to these premises with skepticism—these are, after all, only stories. There are no careful before and after personality measurements documenting positive changes. I will not, for reasons of space, discuss the issues involved in how we know what we know, historical truth versus narrative truth, different forms of causal thinking (probabilistic and narrative), and other complexities. Rather, I ask the reader to assume, at least for the moment, that the narratives of turning points and psychological growth reflect substantial reality. Doing so allows me to move to the next issue—what are the mechanisms or processes that translate these life experiences into psychological growth?

During all of my career and until quite recently, the most common answer to questions about the underlying processes of psychological growth involved the idea of internalization. We are assumed to take in to ourselves those persons (or certain of their characteristics) who we love and who love us in return. The major problem with this concept is that it doesn't tell us much that we need to know. Although Valliant's effort at distinguishing different types of internalization (and their relative maturity) have been helpful at the descriptive level, there remains the mystery of what he calls metabolizing the internalized other (1). What is involved in metabolizing? Is it but a convenient metaphor?

During the last few years several new parameters have been added to the internalization—metabolism model of psychological growth. First, enduring changes in behavior must be associated with actual changes in brain structure and function. New synapses are formed (perhaps also new neurons) as the consequence of life experiences. Thus, psychological growth and brain growth are parallel processes. Second, for synaptogenesis to occur in response to life experiences, previously inactive genes must be "turned on" in order to produce the proteins required in synaptogenesis. Psychological growth, like psychopathology, is thus the product of gene-environment interactions. Nothing very surprising about that. Further, we think we know a good deal about the relationship characteristics that are associated with psychological growth but very little about the actual genes involved. Although it is commonplace to read about "the genes for closeness", "connecting to others is hard-wired," and the like, there are no systematic data.

The relationship structure associated with individual psychological growth was described years ago by our research group at the Timberlawn Research Foundation (2). A major task of relationship formation is establishing a balance of separateness (autonomy) and connectedness (intimacy) acceptable to both partners. In growth-facilitating relationships the partners contribute more or less equally to the process of negotiating a balance suitable to each. Thus, shared power (in defining the relationship) is a crucial variable. This facilitates the development of exploratory conversations that, over time, produce psychological intimacy. Shared power also contributes to the development of the negotiation skills that are crucial for dealing with the inevitable differences. Thus, problem-solving skills come to be highly developed. In all of this, however, each partner maintains a strong capacity for autonomous functioning. The strong interdependence does not erode individuality.

Thus, experiencing such a co-constructed relationship sets the stage for each partner to internalize desirable attributes of the other's. The experience of such relationships—and, perhaps, as suggested by Siegel, in particular the exploratory, intimacy-producing conversations, turns on those genes which are necessary for the production of new synapses (3).

Increasingly we know more useful questions to ask. In this way our understanding of how certain types of relationships appear to facilitate individual growth is gradually expanded.

References

1. Vaillant, G. (1993). *The Wisdom of the Ego.* Cambridge, MA: Harvard University Press.
2. Lewis, J.M., Beavers, W.R., Gossett, JT, Phillips VA. (1976). *No Single Thread: Psychological Health in Family Systems.* New York: Brunner-Mazel.
3. Siegel, DJ. (1999). *The Developing Mind: Toward a Neurobiology of Interpersonal Experience.* New York: The Guilford Press.

February 2007

7

FROM SIBLING DIFFERENCES TO INTERNAL REPRESENTATIONS

They were as different as can be imagined. The older brother, only 18 months senior, was much the quieter more structured and disciplined, had fewer friends, and seemed content to be alone. The younger brother was far more spontaneous, expressive of feelings, affectionate, and had a larger circle of friends. These differences were obvious from early childhood and seemed to account for their different developmental trajectories. The older brother was far the better student and went on to graduate school. In contrast, the younger brother spent only two years in college, leaving to take a job in sales. At midlife the older brother had a stable professional career and marriage while the younger brother had gone from one sales job to another and was in his third marriage.

Nor surprisingly, their parents and extended family believed that these differences in personality were entirely inherited. The differences were apparent so early in life that it was widely held that their subsequent developmental outcomes flowed directly from their different genetic endowments. After all, what difference could there be in their environment? They were raised by the same parents, lived in the same neighborhoods, went to the same schools, and had the same opportunities.

This formulation—sibling differences as a result of only genetic differences—has been shown to be a simplistic and misleading reductionism. What is surprising, perhaps, is that the challenge to this reductionism has come, to a considerable extent, from research aimed to study how differences in genetic makeup account for differences in siblings' personalities. Quantitative behavioral genetics relies on a methodology in which the personalities (and development of psychiatric disorders) are compared in siblings of different degrees of genetic relatedness (twins, adopted siblings, etc.) raised together or apart. A large number of studies have demonstrated that sibling differences arise from three categories of variables; genetic, shared environmental influences, and nonshared environmental factors. In addition to documenting the role of genetic factors in personality, these studies have consistently indicated that nonshared environmental factors play a major role in producing personality differences in siblings.

Nonshared environmental factors are multiple and include differential parental treatment, gender, birth rank order, different experiences of the sibling relationship itself, different peer influences, and the occurrence of such nonsystematic events as illnesses, accidents, and the like. Some of these nonshared environmental factors interact with each other in complex ways. Our own research, for example, suggests that in more functional families sibling rank order is very influential, whereas in more dysfunctional families gender is more decisive. We concluded that the influences of sibling rank order and gender differed as a function of family competence (1). It is to be emphasized, however, that these nonshared environmental factors are assumed to be interwoven with genetic differences: siblings, to a significant extent, do create some of the environmental response through the influence of partially genetically determined personality characteristics.

The attempt to document the exact nature of nonshared environmental factors has proven to be most difficult. David Reiss, the noted family researcher, and his colleagues, for example, have reported the results of a monumental longitudinal study of adolescent development that, by its sheer scope, surpasses most other developmental studies (2). They studied over 700 families containing two same-sexed siblings who were four or fewer years apart, and they studied them on two occasions separated by a three-year interval. Following the procedures of quantitative behavioral genetics, the two adolescent siblings were of different degrees of genetic relatedness (from monozygotic twins to adopted siblings who have no genetic relatedness). What is most impressive about this study, however, is that environmental influences—at least those operating within the family—were directly observed and measured using state of the art interactional techniques. Thus, this research project was carefully designed to inform about nonshared environmental influences (as well as genetic and shared environmental influences).

The reported results add much to our understanding of adolescent development. The important role of genetic influences was documented. The earlier results from quantitative behavioral genetic research that suggested a modest, if any, role for shared environmental influences were contradicted. Shared environmental influences (e.g. stable family characteristics) account for a significant part of adolescent personality in crucial areas such as autonomy and sociability.

Even in this remarkable study, however, the nature of the nonshared environmental influences—a very significant contributor to personality differences—remains elusive. The data supplied do not inform about what these factors are. Reiss discusses this surprising turn of events in a careful manner and makes a cogent case that the answer may be in the psychoanalytic concept of internal representations of self and others. In other words, the manner in which experiences are taken into the self, stored, recalled, and narrated is believed to be a highly individualistic process. Two siblings could internalize the same experiences within the family or in their social world in very different ways, and these differences in representations could play important roles in personality development and consequent sibling differences. Reiss also discusses the fact that, although techniques have been developed to identify internal representations, his study's methodology (e.g., a sample of over 700 families and 1400 adolescents) did not include the opportunity to conduct the intensive interviews and other measures necessary to identify internal representations.

This step, however, has recently been described in another remarkable longitudinal study (3). Sroufe and his colleagues report on individuals from adverse socio-economic circumstances who were studied from birth into young adulthood. These investigators describe the development of age-appropriate techniques to get at the nature of the individual's internal representations. What is very exciting in their findings is that these measures of representations substantially predict behavior at the next developmental stage and that experiences at that developmental stage predict the nature of the internal representations at the following developmental stage. Thus, Reiss's conclusion that his project's inability to identify internal representations as part of nonshared environmental influences (not being designed to get at representations) is addressed by Sroufe's longitudinal study of the systematic interplay between internal representations and behavior.

All of this is (or should be) most exciting to clinicians of diverse theoretical orientations. These two remarkable research projects have begun to document the central importance of the ways in which relationships are experienced, stored, recalled, and narrated. Whether we use the language of internal representations, internal working models, cognitive schemata, or core assumptions and expectations, a fundamental clinical premise derived from various psychotherapies is being documented by systematic longitudinal research.

How sweet it is.

References

1. Lewis J.M., et al.(1976). *No Single Thread: Psychological Health in Family Systems.* New York: Brunner/Mazel.
2. Reiss D, et al. (2000). *The Relationship Code,* Cambridge, MA: The Harvard University Press.
3. Sroufe LA, et al (2005). *The Development of the Person: The Minnesota Study of Risk and Adaption From Birth to Adulthood.* New York: The Guilford Press.

May 2006

8

NARRATIVE IDENTITY AND TURNING POINTS

Anita, as I will call her, was referred to me by her internist for what he described as a chronic, treatment-resistant depression. She was a moderately obese, slow moving, and clearly sad middle-aged woman who spoke without affective modulation. She dated the onset of her depression to her husband's death in a small plane crash eight years before our initial appointment. He was described as a dynamic, successful executive who had cared for her in what sounded like a parental way.

"Since Harold's death," she said tearfully, "my life has ended. Everyday is filled with misery. I don't go out—all I do is eat and sleep. I've tried a grief group, antidepressants, and three different therapists, and nothing helps. I feel dead but can't kill myself because of my religion."

The story that Anita reported of her life before her husband's death emphasized safe dependency, limited autonomy, and a high level of life satisfaction. All of that had been taken from her by the loss of her husband.

In striking contrast to Anita's story was that of Helen's (a pseudonym), who was seen for a psychiatric evaluation as part of the ordination process for the Episcopal priesthood. She, too, had lost her husband some years earlier.

Helen, also middle-aged, was a tall, graying woman with a warm smile and direct manner. She described the death of her husband from cancer with clear sadness. "I was devastated," she said, "We had a good marriage; enjoyed so many things together. He was a dear, dear man and his death so early in life challenged everything I believed about life—even who I was. After the initial shock and grief I had to figure out what I was going to do with my life. I realized that before his death I had been very complacent, self-satisfied, and probably selfish. Gradually and with a good deal of uncertainty I began to experiment with a new me, a new life, I think I've become more sensitive to others, maybe even more caring. I find satisfaction in helping others. My outlook on life has also changed. I'm more in touch with the spiritual side of life. My decision to pursue the priesthood seems to be natural and right for who I am now."

There are a number of ways to think about the striking difference in Anita's and Helen's responses to a tragic loss. Some clinicians would emphasize pre-existing differences in ego strength; others would point out the described differences in marital structure. Anita's marriage appeared to support or require her dependency, and Helen's marriage did not. Other clinicians might emphasize that Helen's loss occurred over time: She had the time for anticipatory grieving. Anita's loss was a sudden lightening strike—there was no time for her to ready herself. Other clinicians would postulate that Anita had a genetic loading for depression that Helen did not share. These clinical perspectives are all useful and, perhaps, are most often combined in a clinical formulation.

In this column, however, I wish to use the difference in Anita's and Helen's outcome to illustrate another and rapidly emerging clinical perspective—that of narrative identity and the role of turning points in the construction of narrative identity. In what follows I am particularly indebted to the empirical studies of McAdams whose results are reported in publications not usually read by psychiatrists (see, for example, references 1 and 2).

McAdams suggests that three complimentary perspectives are available in understanding the person. The first, personality traits, are those enduring dispositions that have relative freedom from context. The second, contextualized characteristics (e.g. roles, defense mechanisms, values) differentiate and enrich descriptions of a person. The third, narrative identity, refers to the individual's life story, the constantly revised narrative that provides unity and meaning to the person's life.

Life stories almost invariably contain one or several turning points (nuclear episodes) that reflect the themes of power (competence, influence, status) and intimacy (relationships, love, caring). Some turning points involve power, others intimacy, and others both power and intimacy. Some turning points are termed "redemptive" in that good comes out of bad. Others are called "contaminating" because something negative arises from a beginning state of goodness. Anita's life story is clearly that of a contaminating sequence, whereas Helen's is obviously redemptive.

What is important to recognize is that life stories are not the simple rendition of the facts of one's life; rather, they arise out of the construction of a narrative that includes but is not restricted to the facts. This, despite the observation that individuals believe their stories are factual and are often resistant to the idea that considerable reconstruction has occurred.

In dealing with turning points, the emphasis is that persons attend some of the consequences of the event and neglect others. These differences in what is attended to are considered an aspect of the person's narrative strategy. Persons with higher levels of ego development have been shown to be more likely to use redemptive strategies in dealing with negative events than are those with less mature ego functioning. At the same time the use of a redemptive narrative strategy is thought to enhance ego functioning. Recall that although Helen likely had a more mature level of ego functioning than Anita, her use of a redemptive strategy in dealing with the loss of her husband appeared to have led over time to a different sense of herself, a more caring relationship pattern, and a revised system of personal meaning. These consequences, of course, are the hallmarks of adult transformation and stand in sharp contrast to Anita's chronic depression.

We do not understand all that is involved in developing narrative strategies. The level of ego maturation is certainly one factor. Another approach treats the ability to find good in bad as something like a personality trait called "benefit finding" (3). There is a growing empirical literature demonstrating that those who can perceive benefits in adversity do better in coping with a wide variety of severe illnesses and negative life circumstances. How directly narrative strategies are influenced by the individual's level of cognitive development needs exploration. It seems reasonable that higher levels of cognition involving the capacity to deal with multiple variables, complex interactions, and probabilistic outcomes would directly influence the development of narrative strategies for dealing with life events. The complex interface between defense mechanisms and narrative strategies obviously needs study.

I have found this large body of empirical work a helpful perspective in treating some patients. Currently, for example, I am working with a middle-aged woman who was abused by her mother throughout childhood. Her response to her mother beating her was to endure silently. Crying out or responding aggressively resulted in her mother's intensified violence. Despite these early circumstances she had achieved a great deal. She is a successful professional, has a stable, satisfactory marriage, and her two young adult children are doing well. In her family life and work she demonstrates the ability to care for others. Despite these considerable accomplishments, she continues to struggle with feeling good about herself. There is an underlying self-critical and depressive theme in her life story identity. We work together to understand better why she clings to the negative messages of her internalized abusive mother rather than adopt the heroic perspective her life story warrants. In this work there is the clear implication of her potential for agency and choice. She has, however, yet to learn that active responses, taking charge of her life story is really safe. In her relationship to herself she remains the abused and passive little girl for whom an active response is dangerous.

At a personal level the perspective of narrative identity with its turning points is a useful way of summing up during later years. Years ago time spent at the Brigham in Boston was a turning point for me in that I recognized that most of my colleagues appeared interested in what seemed a narrow band of emerging basic science. I (and a few others) were more intrigued with the stories we heard from patients, the ways in which their life narratives seemed both implicated in and altered by their illnesses. This was the real beginning of a change in career direction from internal medicine to psychiatry. It was not an easy change because my family, friends, and mentor disapproved. Like other turning points, over time it changed my sense of self, my narrative identity.

References

1. McAdams, Dan P. (1988). *Power, Intimacy, and the Life Story: Personological Inquiries into Identity*. New York: Guilford Press.
2. McAdams, Dan P., Reynolds, Jeffrey, Lewis, Martha, Patten, Allison H., Bowman, Phillip J. (2001). "When Bad Things Turn Good and Good Things Turn Bad: Sequences of Redemption and Contamination in Life Narratives and Their Relation to Psychosocial Adaptation in Midlife Adults and /or Students." Personality and Social Psychology Bulletin, 27:4, April, pp. 474-485.
3. Affleck, G. and Tenner, H. (1996). "Construing Benefits From Adversity: Adaptational Significance and Dispositional Underpinnings." Journal of Personality, 64, pp. 899-922.

July 2003

9

POSTTRAUMATIC GROWTH SYNDROME: FACT OR FICTION?

She was 57, widowed with two grown children, and being evaluated as an aspirant for the Episcopal diaconate. An open, warm, and articulate woman, she described the major turning point in her life as her husband's sudden cardiac death when he was 42 and she 37. "It came out of the blue," she said, "one moment he was here and the next moment he was gone."

Her grief was unremitting and after over two years she began psychotherapy with a psychiatrist who also prescribed an antidepressant. "He said I had a major depression—no energy, couldn't sleep, and continued to cry much of the time." Her recovery was gradual, and she described it in the following way: "The therapy helped, but several different antidepressants didn't seem to do anything but cause side effects. What really made a crucial difference was mostly spiritual." She went on to describe the support received from her priest and congregation and an intensification of her previous religious belief system centering about a deeper relationship with God.

Although her major depression did not totally remit for four years, she has been symptom-free for 16 years. Indeed, she believes that she has been functioning at a higher level psychologically than ever before. "I think I'm more confident and independent than when I was married, and I also believe I'm better with people—more empathic and caring. I look forward to formalizing my helping by becoming an ordained deacon."

Over one fourth of the interviewed Episcopal aspirants described a severe life crisis and its resolution as a significant part of their callings. Most of them described dysfunctional families of origin, often severely so and with experienced physical and/or sexual abuse. Many had histories of sequential relationship failures. Although this group of nonclinical subjects emphasized the spiritual component of their recovery and experienced growth, my earlier in-depth interviews with research volunteer subjects revealed a significant minority who also described prior major life crises (most often major depression) recovery, and self-experienced psychological growth without noting a spiritual component.

In this essay the focus will be on what to make of self-reported growth following trauma. As will become clear, there are two opposing views in those who study the aftermath of serious trauma. One holds that having experienced growth as a consequence of trauma is an illusion that is central and helpful to the process of coping. The opposing view is that the reported growth is real, that the changes reported are accurate accounts of changes in the self.

The published literature on this topic is huge, and anything like a comprehensive review is not possible in this essay. Rather, I write about the topic because much of what is written is not published in journals usually read by clinicians. Further, many clinicians are appropriately concerned with the post-traumatic stress syndrome, how to better understand and treat this often devastating disorder. There is also the issue of sampling: clinicians see patients and not nonclinical subjects whose life narratives are more likely to contain accounts of psychological growth through adversity and suffering. Finally, there is the concern that acknowledging that some students of trauma believe that the self-reported growth is real may in some way be used to demean those who develop post-traumatic stress syndromes.

The position of those who endorse the coping perspective is illustrated by the work of Janoff-Bulman (1). She is a major theoretician of trauma and its consequences and reports on her own research and that of others. Her major stance is cognitive—social. All persons, to one extent or another, hold basic assumptions (conscious or unconscious beliefs) about themselves, the external world, and the relationship between the two. The three fundamental assumptions are that one's personal world is basically benevolent; that life makes sense (order and meaning), and that one is worthy and in control. It is these core assumptions that are overturned by severe and especially random trauma, and it is the struggle to redo these adaptive illusions that is at the core of the coping process. It is the confrontation with one's own survival—whether resulting from serious accidents, natural disasters, disease, or criminal attacks—that is the defining feature of the trauma. One is forced to recognize one's deepest vulnerability. In taking this position Janoff-Bulman adopts an overtly existential stance. Denial and intrusive recollections are considered—within certain limits—to have adaptive value. They are often part of the coping process allowing the victim to work gradually on reconstituting a changed assumptive world. For some survivors the need to talk—to become the active storyteller—can also be understood as adaptive.

There are also three major cognitive strategies: comparing their experiences favorably with real or imagined other victims is one. A second is an element of self-blame. Here a distinction is made between characterological self-blame and the transient self-blame that reflects an adaptive effort to reduce the randomness (and meaninglessness) of the traumatic event.

The third cognitive strategy is finding some benefit in the traumatic experience. Most commonly these self-interpretations involve lessons about life (how precious it is) and lessons about the self (I am now more compassionate and caring). Such interpretations are adaptive in the sense that they help in restoring meaning to life.

Janoff-Bulman's data support the fact that most trauma victims recover in the sense of re-establishing a new and reasonably comfortable assumptive world that incorporates their dreadful experience. The trauma is, however, permanently encoded. Some degree of disillusionment remains. Thus, this body of careful research and complex theorizing ends on a positive note. It is not, however, the "better than before" that is central to the concept of post-traumatic growth.

The opposite view—that the changes reported following trauma are real, that there is a post-traumatic growth syndrome—is supported by equally competent researchers and theorists. The example I shall use here is the work of Tedeschi (2). He emphasizes that the suffering and struggle resulting from the trauma is necessary for growth to occur. The empirical evidence for growth is supported by the sameness of reported changes across many studies. These are a changed sense of self in which, for example, one is both and paradoxically more vulnerable and more self-reliant; a greater emphasis on empathic, caring relationships with others; and a changed perspective on the meaning of life.

Tedeschi also suggests that certain personality characteristics predispose some persons to grow as a result of their struggle with trauma. Dispositional optimism, cognitive complexity, internal locus of control, and extraversion are emphasized. He speculates that the relationship between personality and growth through adversity may be curvilinear—that is, it is neither those with very high or very low levels of pertinent personality characteristics who are most likely to grow.

For the most part Tedeschi emphasizes the same crucial coping processes as Janoff-Bulman does. The ultimate outcome is determined by the repair of cognitive schema (adaptive illusions) and the reworking of a life narrative in which the trauma and response occupy a central place. He writes, "There is nothing new or remarkable in the assertion that psychological growth can be precipitated by the pain of unfortunate events. What we have found new and remarkable is how often this happens and how apparently ordinary people achieve extraordinary wisdom through their struggle with circumstances that are initially aversive in the extreme" (2, p. 2).

One of the problems for clinicians is how to interpret these different views. There are systematic studies that support both positions. Tennen and Affleck can be recommended for a thoughtful and balanced overview (3). They believe that there are too many unanswered questions about the concept of post-traumatic growth to come to a definitive answer. Longitudinal studies (with their possibility of pretrauma measurements) are badly needed. There remains much to learn about personality predispositions, sudden versus gradual change, the reported gender differences (women more likely to report benefits and growth), and those aspects of personality that struggling with trauma may change.

In the beginning of this essay I emphasized that the voluminous literature about this topic is mostly reported in journals and books not ordinarily read by clinicians whose major focus is on the post-traumatic stress syndrome. The purpose of this essay is to call to the attention of clinicians that there is a vigorous and ongoing academic debate involving suffering and its consequences. The old adage that what doesn't kill you makes you stronger continues to attract the attention of serious students of trauma and its consequences.

References

1. Janoff-Bulman, R. (1992). *Shattered Assumptions: Towards a New Psychology of Trauma.* New York: The Free Press.
2. Tedeschi, R.G., Calhoun, L.G. (1995). *Trauma & Transformation: Growing in the Aftermath of Suffering.* California: Sage Publications.
3. Tennen, H., Affleck, G. (1998). "Personality and Transformation in the Face of Adversity" in the *LEA Series in Personality and Clinical Psychology.* New Jersey: Erlbaum.

December 2007

10

THE ROADS LESS TRAVELED

A forty-year-old man described a near-death experience in the intensive care unit of a local hospital. He had been a homeless alcoholic for six years and was discovered under a bridge with hypothermia, pneumonia, and close to death. The near-death experience involved the out-of-the-body experience, the bright light, the tunnel, and other typical aspects of this dramatic narrative. When he recovered he joined AA, pursued an education, and has now worked effectively for 12 years in a well-known program for the homeless.

A 52 year-old woman described the dramatic change in her life after participating in a two-week silent retreat 10 years ago. During the retreat she explored with herself the numerous contradictions that had characterized her life. Her inability to commit to a relationship, marked vocational instability, drug abuse, and other markers of a chaotic lifestyle came to be understood as reflecting underlying conflicts between love and hate, omnipotence and powerlessness, self-centeredness and altruism, and other basic internal contradictions. In the several months following the retreat she brought herself under behavioral control, found a job in a social agency, and several years later entered a stable marriage that is now in its eighth year.

A 26 year-old senior medical student described an intense spiritual experience during his undergraduate days. During his

> sophomore year he was drinking heavily, failing most of his courses, and was quite reclusive. One day while drowsing in bed he experienced a several minute period of intense emotionality, profound peacefulness, and the sense of floating through space. He interpreted the experience as spiritual although he saw no visions nor heard any voices. "Most of all," he said, "There was the feeling of oneness—of deep connection to all of nature." In the following months he stopped drinking, began studying, and reached out to form a supportive social network. In the years following he has married, fathered a child, and done well in medical school.

The opportunity to spend several hours exploring the life stories of nonclinical subjects can be an enlightening experience for a psychotherapist. During the last three decades I have had hundreds of such opportunities with applicants for a psychiatric residency, volunteers for marital-family research, and, more recently, postulants for the Episcopal priesthood. A few of these subjects reported a decisive turning point in their lives; an experience that changed them—often dramatically—for the better. What had been lives filled with chaos and despair were transformed to lives of purpose and meaning. Often their new identities were characterized by the major theme of altruism, a pervasive caring for others that replaced an earlier and profound self-centeredness. Further, the changes appeared to be long-lasting and stable.

After hearing a small number of accounts of these sudden, dramatic, and apparently lasting changes in adult behavior, I decided to review the relevant literature, a process that continues to this day. It is convenient to categorize these experiences, and, currently my categories include near-death experiences, "quantum" changes, spiritual and religious experiences, single encounters with others, drug experiences, solitude, "spontaneous" recovery from severe psychiatric disorders, and group experiences. This literature is mostly anecdotal, but gradually more systematic descriptive studies are appearing. It is far too early in my quest to even speculate about underlying commonalities; the purpose of this essay is much different. I wish to explore several of the reasons why I and presumably other mental health professionals have resisted taking seriously such transformations.

The first reason is that the practice of clinical disciplines fills our professional lives with patients who have not had such experiences. Or, perhaps, we are not in the habit of asking about them. I can recall only one such report from a psychotherapy patient—and she and her husband were seen in couples therapy. Further, her spontaneous account came about only after she learned of my interest. Each of the other eight accounts came from nonclinical subjects.

A second reason involves our lack of agreement on what is "real." I can still recall the pounding I took as a resident when I presented the case of a young woman I saw in the teaching clinic. She was a hospital staff member and had been seen psychotherapeutically over the years by a number of those in attendance at the presentation. Her symptoms were markedly resistant to both psychotherapy and the then available psychotropic drugs. After our fifth session she reported a dramatic clearing of her symptoms, and I was at a loss to explain how her change related to anything that had transpired in our few sessions. The pounding I took was couched in the language of "flight into health;" her changes were not real. I have no long-term follow-up, although nine months later when I finished my training, she remained symptom-free.

I have come to believe that sudden transformations are real if, in addition to the clearing of symptoms, the new behaviors are consistent with what is known about adult ego maturation. Thus, one listens for evidence that prior immature mechanisms of defense have been replaced by altruism, anticipation, and the other mature defense mechanisms.

A third reason for our collective inattention involves the idea that sudden and dramatic changes do not fit the prevalent theory of how adult maturation occurs. Maturation is thought to be a slow process of incremental change, most often in the context of an intense relationship. The key mechanism is the internalization of the desirable qualities of the important other. This perspective remains dominant despite the slipperiness of the concept of internalization. This view of adult maturation leads to grave doubt about the validity of changes that are sudden and dramatic and do not involve an important relationship. Let me illustrate with something I heard some years ago about religious conversions. It was said that of every hundred converts of a well-known evangelist only five would report sustained life change one year later and but one of the hundred sustained those changes five years later. Although these figures speak to something of the transience of conversion effects for most, there has been, I believe, little interest in systematically studying the few for whom religious conversion resulted in enduring changes. Such sudden and dramatic changes do not fit the prevalent model of adult maturation.

Finally, there is the cultural belief that anything good must come through hard work. Sudden, dramatic changes without sustained effort are suspect; blood, sweat, and tears are required.

There are doubtlessly other factors that add to our collective resistance to consider seriously that adult maturation can occur—at least for some—in ways that are sudden, dramatic, and lasting. It is, I believe, a sign of our maturation as a clinical discipline that there is increased interest in the serious study of such different roads to adult maturation.

September 2002

11

CALLINGS

"Tell me about your calling."

"It's not easy to describe. Some years ago my wife divorced me — said I was a workaholic, never truly there for her. I got very depressed and was miserable—could hardly get out of bed, and my productivity as a broker fell drastically. Saw a therapist, took an antidepressant, and that helped—but I still wasn't myself. Gradually, I began to feel that God wanted something else from me, and the idea of becoming a priest came to occupy more and more of my thoughts. It seemed that, for all of my economic success, I had been terribly self-centered and needed to redirect my life. I began to visit with my priest, and, after a while, he suggested I consider studying for the deaconate. I started then and here I am six years later a candidate for ordination for the priesthood. I feel like a different person, like God has called me to do what I've been meant to do."

"So, in your early forties, you were very successful as a broker, but after your wife divorced you, you got really depressed and coming out of that crisis has changed the whole direction of your life. And, although the therapy and medication helped, it was the experience of being called that really turned things around."

"Yes, those are the bare bones of it. Another important part of it, though, is several years ago I met a woman, and she and I love each other and share a deep spirituality."

This middle-aged man described a severely dysfunctional family of origin involving abuse from his alcoholic father and a history of failed relationships throughout his adult years. Although economically successful, he was without a coherent system of meaning until the emergence from depression appears to have initiated a process of personality re-organization and apparent growth.

As this essay is written I am reviewing the evaluation interviews with 88 candidates for ordination in the Episcopal denomination. One aspect of my semistructured interview format involves exploring each candidate's experience of a calling. At its most inclusive level a calling has been defined as a strong, inner impulse to a particular course of action or duty (1). From this perspective a calling does not always involve religious vocations; one can be called to other occupations including medicine. A literature review has revealed that, despite the huge literature on science and religion with significant attention paid to the psychology of conversion, there is practically nothing published on the psychology of callings.

Thus, there is much to learn. As, for example, are persons with certain personality characteristics more apt to experience a calling? What is the natural history of a calling? Is a calling a relatively brief experience or a lifelong part of the self? What experiences over time influence the processes involved in the course of a calling? Such questions only begin to probe the unknowns about the psychology of a calling.

There appear to be multiple adult experiences that may initiate adult psychological growth. "Healing" marriages, psychotherapy, religious conversions, dealing with adversity, meditation, and others are only some of the examples. A calling may also be an experience that initiates or reflects psychological growth. Interview studies—such as my evaluation interviews with 88 candidates—can be seen as qualitative research, a necessary beginning that may yield hypotheses to be tested by more rigorous quantitative studies.

In this essay, however, I wish to use another source of data about callings—my personal experience of a calling to medicine and, later, psychiatry. Understanding such personal experiences may also lead to useful hypotheses about the psychology of callings. The specific nature of my experiences is not what I believe to be generalizable; rather, it is that the callings occur in a particular developmental context, involve the resolution of conflict, and are aided by support from an important other.

It was, during adolescence that I began to feel "the strong inner impulse" to become a doctor. The "impulse" was actually more like a conviction that being a doctor was what I wanted my life to involve. It was as if I had come upon an important self-observation, and it was an exciting, positive experience. As I began to let people know that this decision had been made, the feedback was almost always positive. The lone and important exception was my father. A powerful, charismatic man who had achieved much with but a high school education, he had other plans for me. A major turning point in his own young adult life was a World War I commission and a decorated battle career that brought about much social acceptance not earlier found as a poor farm boy. The worst experience of his life was being discharged after that war—much against his wishes—when only West Point graduates were retained. It came, then, as no surprise that he wanted me to go to West Point to fulfill his dream.

I was ambivalent—wanting to please him but not at all sure that a military career was right for me. He obtained an appointment for me, but I flunked the then rigorous visual examination. My calling to medicine thus occurred in the familiar adolescent developmental challenge of establishing an identity, one that was centered on my wishes rather than on pleasing a powerful parent. Put in a different way, I needed a calling to resolve an underlying conflict with my father and to fortify my emerging autonomy.

Support for my calling came mostly from my mother. She idealized doctors and was thrilled with my choice. I believe her feelings of approval were genuine but probably also influenced by her use of indirect oppositionalism with her powerful spouse.

The sense of calling to psychiatry had some similarities. It began as an intern at the Brigham in Boston. I did well and my professors outlined the steps leading to a possible academic career there. Now a young adult husband and father-to-be, the ultimate career decision had to be made. Most of my house staff colleagues planned academic careers but, when asked what in academic medicine they wished to pursue, responded with what seemed like narrow interests. One mentioned several amino acids, another the pancreas. In contrast, I found myself increasingly interested in patients' stories—what are now called illness narratives. Psychiatrists were assigned to each of the medical wards and were freely available to discuss such matters as well as one's responses to patients and their stories. Although I did not experience a calling to psychiatry then (that took several years), I did become aware of the conflict about where I thought academic internal medicine was going and my basic interests.

Boston medicine in the early 50's was more favorably inclined toward psychoanalysis and psychiatry than my young medical school in Dallas and the physicians I knew in practice. A career in psychiatry came to be seen by me as not necessarily a second rate option; rather a specialty that attracted some of the best and brightest. I am certain that the intellectual ambiance of Boston academic medicine impacted my growing conflict.

Not surprisingly, however, my relationship with another powerful man was involved. Tinsley R. Harrison (Harrison's Principles of Internal Medicine) was at the new Dallas medical school while I was a student. He selected one or two medical students each year to take a year out of school and become his personal research fellows. I did so and the experience with him changed my life in many ways. He was a remarkable teacher, one of the last bedside clinicians of prominence in academic medicine, and a learned, charismatic mentor. There was no question in my mind that I wanted to follow his example, and he was unstinting in his warm support of those plans. I was to train in Boston and then return to work with him.

It was, once again, in the context of the strong need to please an older, powerful, and charismatic man who had given so much to me that my calling to psychiatry began to grow. Once again, it was experienced as a growing inner conviction that this career pathway was "right" for me. I reminded myself that literature and the humanities always had more appeal than chemistry and biology. Family and friends in Texas were polite but clearly unenthusiastic when I began to talk about going into psychiatry. My wife supported my decision, although much later revealing that it involved some discomfort for her. Harrison offered only a type of ambivalent support when I finally told him. "Wonderful," he said, "Get your psychiatric training then a year or so in the cath lab here with me, and then we'll talk about a division of psychosomatic medicine." He wasn't going to let go.

These reflections about my sense of being called to medicine, then psychiatry suggest that the psychology of a calling may, for some, include a developmental challenge involving the conflict between establishing an autonomous identity and pleasing important others. The calling itself can be understood psychologically as a resolution of this conflict and the initiation of a period of growth. My experiences (and those of the Episcopal candidates I have interviewed) also suggest that external support from important others may be a crucial component of responding to the calling.

There are jobs, careers, and callings. We know much more about jobs and careers than we do callings. Bellah and his colleagues, however, have suggested that callings (more than careers or jobs) are much more likely to be incorporated into the basic sense of self (2). If such is so, callings present an unusual opportunity for personality growth. We need, therefore, to understand callings better and perhaps our personal experiences may be one starting point.

References

1. *Webster's Third New International Dictionary*. Springfield, Mass: G. and C. Merriam Co., 1964.
2. Bellah R.N., Madsen R., Sullivan W.M., et al. (1985). *Habits of the Heart: Individualism as Commitment in American Life*. Berkeley, CA: University of California Press.

November 2006

12

DO MEANINGS MATTER?

My father-in-law lived until his late 90s. A hard-working, scantily educated man, he dealt lovingly with me, despite his tacit endorsement of a primary redneck value to never trust a man who works without sweating. Shortly before his death, I asked him what he thought his life had meant. He looked at me with a "what kind of a foolish question is that?" expression and responded, "Damn if I know." Whether he had truly never thought of his life's meaning or was reacting to my intrusiveness is hard to know. My guess is that he really did not think much about such issues, but, if you knew him well, his life's meaning seemed apparent. He did not seem to believe in a personal God and thought that life after death was only a "nice idea." Rather, he believed in family ties, hard work, and being both independent and honorable. These values were not openly articulated but clearly apparent from how he lived his life.

There is only one hint available on how many persons are like my late father-in-law (or my guess about him). One Finnish study reported that five to 30 percent of various samples of the very old (over 80) reported that they could not say if their lives had meaning (1). There are also data indicating that 60 to 80 percent of these samples of older persons are more like me in thinking about and articulating their search for meaning. There are, however, no longitudinal data collected from the same persons across many years to suggest how stable or unstable systems of meaning may be. In looking back at my life, for example, three different belief systems have been involved—each during a particular developmental phase. During childhood the Jesuits tried to educate me, and I accepted without doubt my mother's Catholicism. Later in adolescence reading H.G. Wells' popularizations of evolutionary theory jolted me out of an untroubled, if superficial religiosity, and ushered in a long-lasting love affair with science. Looking back at these decades of young adulthood and early midlife, it seems obvious that it was more than an interest in science, but also a belief system that—given enough time and effort—could explain everything. This naïve, rigid scientism is recalled with more than a little embarrassment. Somewhere in midlife a third and lasting belief system came into being. More existential than anything else, it centers about relationships as the major source of meaning. As can be noted from this brief (and, I am certain, partially reconstructed) summary, my late father-in-law and I were at opposite poles regarding how much we though about life's meaning. The use I wish to make of this presumed difference involves the question of whether it makes any difference and, if so, what is the nature of the differences?

The topic of life's meaning is, of course, a primary issue in existential theory. Yalom discussed the four "ultimate concerns" of existentialism as being the most fundamental issues in the psychological self (2). Two of them (freedom [one constructs his or her own life] and isolation [in the end one is alone]) have received relatively little systematic professional attention. The other two, anxiety about death and concerns about personal meaning, have received much more attention from psychology and psychiatry and each has attracted some research attention.

The most prolific scientific student of meanings in life has been the psychologist, Roy Baumeister (3). In his rich survey of the efforts of many disciplines to study life meanings, he presents an overview, an initial attempt at a synthesis. People, he concludes, require life to make sense in at least four different ways. He calls these the "needs for meaning." The first is purpose, the idea that current activities are clearly related to the future in the form of a goal or goals. The second is value, the belief that one's behaviors are right, good, and justifiable. The third is efficacy—or, perhaps, control. This need involves the belief that one's life is in one's own hands and represents what some have called an "adaptive illusion." The fourth need for meaning is self-worth. Baumeister suggests that people are more secure in their sense that their lives have meaning if there are multiple ways of satisfying each of these four needs.

Baumeister also writes about the development of a "value gap" during the 20th century. The weakening of a shared religious belief system, the decline of an agreed upon code of morality, and the lessened impact of tradition have combined to produce a cultural climate in which shared values are less available. Into this gap has developed an increasing emphasis on the self—who one is, what one has accomplished—as a central value system upon which life's meaning is constructed. Work, for example, is now much more valued for what it brings to the self (rather than to the common good). Relationships, particularly marriage and family, have become the primary value system for more and more persons. (Eighty-nine percent describe these relationships as "vital" sources of meaning, more than any other value base). Even here, however, close relationships have come to be valued more and more for what they bring to the self (happiness, satisfaction, meaning).

Baumeister concludes that meaning must be imposed on life; that modern society offers a wealth of some forms of meaning—but in little bits—and many persons experience anxiety about whether these bits add up to something "suitably big." Further, creating a comprehensive system of meaning out of these bits may be nice as an ideal but in reality is a very difficult task. People, however, appear to live very satisfactory lives without an explicit system of meaning or overall philosophy of life.

In the 15 years since Baumeister's review and synthesis there has been a spurt of psychological research on the topic of life's meaning. A number of interesting questions have been addressed including the relationship of life's meaning to psychological health, personality characteristics, age, ethnicity, and response to psychotherapy. There are several problems with some of this research. One is the overlap in definitions of meaning and health. When, for example, both meaning and adult psychological health are defined, in part, by the capacity to transcend purely self-interests (generativity, altruism, etc.), their positive correlation is of dubious value. This is particularly so in one category of research in which undergraduate students (usually as a requirement in a psychology course) are given a number of paper and pencil tests and the scores are correlated. Such studies are of dubious merit and almost always show, for example, positive correlations between the strength of belief that one's life has meaning and measures of mental health.

There are, however, more useful studies, and, for me, they are those that rely on exploratory or semistructured interviews, have a longitudinal component, and address what subjects can or will tell you about their life's meaning. I use "can" or "will" because Baumeister comments that many persons are more reluctant to discuss the meaning of their lives than they are to talk about the intimate details of their sexual life. At any rate, there are a handful of such studies, and to illustrate some of their findings, consider the following. About one-third of subjects describe their life's meaning using a clearly thought out, integrated system of meaning. Others discuss what gives their lives meaning without describing such a belief system. The issue of whether having an articulated and integrated system of meaning is crucial for high levels of psychological functioning is still debated. There are also findings that suggest that in some ways having an integrated framework is not as important as the belief that one is in the process of fulfilling (or has fulfilled) the premises of that framework. Finally, almost all subjects in some studies place their relationships (spouses, children, families, friends, etc.) at the center of their system of meaning (4). About three of each four subjects emphasize their personal development and/or creativity as also very important. Religious-spiritual issues are noted by about half of such subjects with less than that identifying their relationships with nature or socio-political movements as important sources of life meaning.

Although these and other intriguing findings almost always need replication with more representative samples and tighter research designs, the studies suggest something of what may be gained from looking more closely at broad existential constructs. As yet, however, they do not clearly inform us about any possible meaning to the differences between the ways in which my late father-in-law and I approached the issue of life meaning. It may turn out that his "Damn if I know" works as well as my open searching as far as psychological health is concerned. That, I suspect, would please him.

References

1. Takkinen, S., Ruoppila, I. (2001). "Meaning in Life in Three Samples of Elderly Persons with High Cognitive Functioning." Int'l J Aging and Human Development, Vol. 53 (1) 51-73.
2. Yalom, I.D. (1980). *Existential Psychotherapy*, New York: Basic Books.
3. Baumeister, R.F. (1991). *Meanings of Life*, New York: The Guilford Press.
4. O'Connor, K., Chamberlain, K. (1996). "Dimension of Life Meaning: A Qualitative Investigation at Mid-life." British J of Psychology, 87:461-477.

January 2007

13

WHICH GOD?

God was never mentioned by my teachers or supervisors fifty years ago when I was a resident. Psychoanalytic theory dominated the teaching program and, in retrospect, the silence about God, religious beliefs and activities, and spirituality in general almost certainly reflected in part an unspoken allegiance to Freud and his negativity about religion.

Later, in the early years of practice, a few practitioners began to advertise themselves as "Christian psychiatrists" or "Christian psychologists." I, and some of my colleagues, thought this was an undesirable dilution of psychotherapeutic principles and, perhaps, even a marketing device.

Over the years much has changed. A strong and productive interface has developed between religion and psychology and psychiatry. There has also been a growing interest in understanding belief systems as providing individuals the cognitive structures in which personal meaning can be sought. For many, if not most, Americans belief systems are religious in nature. Personal meaning is found in one's relationship with God. As such, psychotherapists need to respect the religious belief systems of their patients—however different from their own—but also seek to understand their adaptive implications.

All of this change during the years of my career was brought to mind by two recent experiences. One involved a psychotherapeutic session with a 60 year-old man I have been seeing for several years.

The second experience was my reading the recently published Baylor Religious Survey (1).

The patient, abused as a child, was a successful attorney whose solo practice focused on wills and trusts. He was a quiet, self-effacing man with pervasive self-esteem problems. Neither of his two marriages had survived, and his life had been mostly solitary for the past eight years. His only consistent social interaction involved a Bible study group, the members of which shared his fundamentalist religious orientation. During the interview in question he described his belief that the end-time was rapidly approaching. He recounted the details of that anticipated scenario, stopped abruptly, and then said, "You don't believe any of this, do you?"

"Is it important to you that I do?" I responded.

"I know you don't," he said with much finality.

"And how is that for you?" I asked quietly.

"I really wish you believed as I do," he said, "but our work together is very important to me."

"So you value our work but have to struggle with my having a different belief system?"

"Yeah, I wish it was the same," he said sadly.

"I think each of us needs a belief system in which to search for the meaning in our lives. The key issue for me is respecting each other's beliefs," I responded.

"Sometimes I feel that's a cop-out, a way of trying to explain something away," he said without rancor.

"You may be right," I said, "it feels to me more like we're trying to deal openly with some differences—so, hopefully, they won't impede our work together. But, I'm glad you can tell me it feels sometimes like a cop-out to you."

This interchange went on for the remainder of the session. We talked about a number of the implications of different belief systems including feeling connected, managing doubt, and struggling to trust.

Later that day I went over this session in my mind, wondering whether my way of dealing with the differences in our belief systems had been helpful. If memory serves me right, this was one of very few direct explorations of such differences in over 50 years of psychotherapeutic practice. I reassured myself that after two years in therapy he had initiated our exploration and that meant at some level that he was trusting enough to take such a step. I also reminded myself that at a purely psychological level I believed his belief system—with its promise of being chosen—and his Bible study group were for him important adaptive processes. It also seemed impressive that he could confront my efforts to change the focus (from his theological end-time to my psychological tolerance) as a cop-out. Most of all I hoped that my responses had been as respectful as they needed to be.

He did not re-introduce the topic during subsequent sessions. There is no obvious evidence of a change in our working alliance, and, at the time of this writing, I continue to be watchful. There are no guidelines, however, about dealing with such complex issues.

It was, therefore, with much interest that I read the Baylor Religious Survey (1). Based on a nationally representative sample of 1721 persons' responses to a nearly 400-item questionnaire, the survey is said to be the most extensive ever accomplished.

It is interesting reading for clinicians. I did not, however, hope for answers to my issues of psychotherapeutic process. Rather, I anticipated helpful data about religious belief systems. In this I was not disappointed. First a brief note about the authors' management of the data. They chose to factor analyze the subjects' responses to 29 of the items having to do with the nature of God. They found two distinct factors: God's level of engagement in one's personal life and world affairs and the extent to which God was believed to be critical and punitive. They next divided their subjects into those high and low on the engagement factor and those high and low on God's criticalness. Next they constructed four groups: high engagement—high criticalness (Authoritarian), high engagement—low criticalness—(Benevolent), low engagement—high criticalness (Critical), low engagement—low criticalness (Distant). Although this approach to managing data is common and well accepted in many of the social sciences, there are clinicians who believe its major concern is numbers and not people and as such, tells us little, if anything, about the real lives of real persons. With this caveat in mind, what do these different ways of thinking about God reveal?

The Authoritarian concept of God (31% of the sample) involves the belief that God is highly involved in both one's personal life and world events. He punishes those who do not follow his mandates. The Bible is factual and an infallible guide to life. Subjects with this orientation are more likely to have less education and income and to be women, Blacks, and evangelical Protestants. They are also more likely to believe that premarital sex and abortion are always wrong. As a group they also are more supportive of the present administration and the war in Iraq.

Those with the Benevolent concept of God (23%) also believe that God is very involved in both one's personal life and world affairs, but emphasize His loving nature rather than His punitiveness. They also are less likely to be Biblical literalists. In other ways (demographic, moral premises, and political conservatism) they are much like those with an Authoritarian orientation.

The Critical orientation (16%) involves a God who is distant and uninvolved in personal affairs or world events but does punish (in another life) those who have not followed His precepts. Persons with this orientation are less apt to be absolute about moral issues and tend to follow a less conservative political philosophy.

The Distant concept of God (24%) involves those who believe God is a force in nature (rather than the "He" often endorsed by the other groups). As a group, persons with this orientation are more likely to be better educated men with higher incomes and more liberal political orientations. In these ways they are much like the five percent of the sample who defined themselves as atheists.

Although there is not much surprising in these data, they do add an empirical foundation to that which many have surmised. The data also help locate my patient among those whose concept of God is Authoritarian in that He will punish nonbelievers during the end-time. One way of understanding the adaptive significant of my patient's belief system is to put it in the context of his childhood relationship with an abusive father who never expressed acceptance or affection. The patient's belief system involves a dangerous God who does, however, accept and love him. This interpretive stance reflects Rizzuto's writings about the parental origins of concepts (and internal representations) of God (2).

All of this underscores the importance for psychotherapists to be attentive to differences in belief systems, to reflect genuine respect for those that differ from their own, and to think through the ways in which belief systems may have adaptive significance.

References

1. "American Piety in the 21st Century: New Insights to the Depth and Complexity of Religion in the US." Selected Findings from the Baylor Religion Survey, Conducted by the Baylor Institute for Studies of Religion and Department of Sociology, Baylor University, Sep, 2006.
2. Rizzuto, A.M. (1979). *The Birth of the Living God: A Psychoanalytic Study*. Chicago: University of Chicago Press.

April 2007

14

A BEGINNING BIOLOGY OF BELIEFS?

The idea that there may be genetic influences on how we think about God and politics is usually greeted with disbelief, even scorn. "Ludicrous," was the intense response of a distinguished psychologist-friend upon hearing me explore this topic in a brief paper. It seems that most persons hold dearly to the idea that their religious and political ideologies are freely chosen—that genes have nothing to do with basic belief systems. That has been my position, at least until twin studies began to suggest that hereditary factors influence personality traits and that personality traits influence the choice of ideologies. It is important to emphasize, however, that those investigators whose findings suggest that genetic factors impact ideologies believe that they are but one piece of a complex interaction in which experiential variables usually dominate. The issue is not do genes determine ideologies: rather, do they play any role at all.

The findings regarding both religious and political ideologies emerge from twin studies and focus most firmly on the conservative-liberal dimension of belief systems. There are problems with both twin studies and this major focus. I will deal with them in a bit, but first what are the findings?

Twin studies compare similarities and differences in monozygotic and dyzygotic twins. If monozygotic twins are more alike than dyzygotic twins, the interpretation is that genetic factors account for the difference, and the magnitude of the difference indicates their strength. Two of the better known American twin studies included self-report measures of religious conservatism and found that monozygotic twins were significantly more alike in this characteristic than dyzygotic twins (1, 2). They concluded that genetic factors appear to play an appreciable role in the adoption of conservative religious beliefs. More recently political scientists analyzed the data from one of these studies (involving 8,000 sets of twins) and concluded that the conservative-liberal dimension of political ideologies also has a genetic component (3). Thus, it seems that we should, at a minimum, begin to take the question of genetic influences on ideologies with some seriousness.

If such influences operate they do so most likely indirectly—that is through the genetic impact on personality characteristics. In a more formal way the proposition would be that certain personality characteristics are the mediators of the genetic influence on ideologies. This, of course, means accepting the premise that personality influences choice of ideology, and this proposition has its own up and down history. Jost, in a recent and thorough survey and integration of his own research and that of others, traces the history of academic psychology's phasic acceptance and rejection of the role of personality in determining political ideologies (4). He concludes that there is clear and mounting evidence that certain personality traits are associated with the conservative—liberal dimension of political ideologies. Although there is considerable variation among those who define themselves as either conservative or liberal, three out of each four Americans will do so (self-defined conservatives are over twice as prevalent as their liberal neighbors).

More to the point of this essay, however, is Jost's finding that certain personality traits are more often found in each group. Conservatives, for example, are more apt to demonstrate (again, self-report) a propensity for order, structure, closure, conscientiousness, and tradition. Liberals more often define themselves as open to new experiences, creative, and more tolerant of ambiguity. Since twin studies have demonstrated that most (perhaps all) personality traits have a genetic component, we have a possible connection between genes and political ideologies.

There remain, however, significant questions. The first involves the twin methodology. Although this method continues to be broadly accepted, critics have questioned whether recruitment methods result in a representative sample of twins. Another is how much the twin methodology minimizes environmental influences by assuming, for example, that living in the same family means having the same environment. There is evidence that children in the same family may experience the family differently and that their views change over time. Finally, the results of twin studies only result in information about that particular sample of twins and cannot be safely generalized to other populations. There are other questions about twin studies, and so it seems wise to maintain some degree of skepticism if all the data about genes and ideology come solely from twin studies.

There are also questions about the use of the conservative—liberal dimension as a (or the) defining marker of an ideology. Whether doing so embraces an overly simple reductionism of a much more complex phenomena (belief systems) is a reasonable question. Why not use, for example, complexity, level of integration, or change and stability over time can be asked. Heather Looy has discussed this issue and others in her review of the implications of both evolutionary theory and behavioral genetics (twin studies) for faith (Christian). (5) She comments that people of faith can be uncomfortable with the idea that their beliefs are rooted in their biology—as if something sacred is being degraded. The twin studies, she writes, provide only faint hints about a possible biology of religion. Looy is critical of the attempts to reduce the complexity of religion to easily measured variables and notes the conservative—liberal distinction as one such effort.

Another confounding factor is how the premise that genetic factors influence ideologies accounts for changes in ideology during the adult years. Although I am unaware of any longitudinal data, surely many persons' ideologies are changed (even reversed) by adult experiences. A now-deceased high school friend of mine is an example. He was the son of Sicilian immigrants, lost his mother when he was three years old, and developed an obvious compulsive personality structure that served him well in the world of commerce. Until he was well into his 60s he was a staunch conservative. Then he became increasingly dissatisfied with the outcome of local, state, and national conservative governments. After several years struggle with this issue, he began to articulate a liberal ideology. "I can't believe what's happened to me politically," he said with obvious passion. "I've ended up endorsing all that I opposed all my life. It's incredible—but it really is the way I think now." He not only changed his political ideology but in the last fifteen years of his life was active in causes usually identified with the liberal position.

My friend remained a fairly compulsive person. Order, structure, closure, conscientiousness, and tradition were obvious to the end of his life. I do not know, as I write this, whether my sense that he developed a greater tolerance for doubt and ambiguity, greater support for innovation (as, for example, in healthcare), and more concern about social inequities reflects actual changes in his personality or my reading in such changes because they are "suppose" to mediate his ideological change.

One can reach out further into speculative realms by asking if such changes reflect turning on or off certain genes and the growth of new brain circuits. With these and other obvious issues in mind, the question that can be raised is, "What does all of this have to do with clinical practice?"

I would respond that at this point in time and with only the hint of a possible gene - personality traits—religious and political ideologies interaction, the major implication for clinical practice is in how clinicians think. For most of us it likely is a challenge to broaden our theories of mental function—to allow for a greater variety of causative variables. In short, if these hints are expanded into a more solid data base, we, as clinicians, need to become more flexible in our thinking. And that, we have much reason to believe, will impact how we understand and treat our patients.

References

1. Waller, N.G., Kojetin, B.A., Bouchard, Jr., T.H., Lykken, D.T., Tellegen, A, (1990). "Genetic and Environmental Influences on Religious Interests, Attitudes, and Values." Psychological Science, 1:2, March.
2. D'Onofrio, B.M., Eaves, L.J., Murrelle, L., Wines, H.H., Spika, B. (1999). "Understanding Biological and Social Influence on Religious Affliction, Attitudes and Behaviors." J of Personality, 67:6, 953-984.
3. Jost, J.T. (2006). "The End of the End of Ideology." American Psychologist, October.
4. Alford, J.R., Funk, C.L., Hibbing, J.R. (2005). "Are Political Orientations Genetically Transmitted?" Am Political Science Review, 99, 153-167.
5. Looy, H. (2005). "The Body of Faith: Genetic and Evolutionary Considerations." Journal of Psychology and Christianity, 24:2, 113-121.

February 2008

15

HOW TO GET IN THE MAINSTREAM

They were both in their 40's and each had the necessary symptoms for a diagnosis of a major depressive disorder. Despite this similarity, they were as different as day and night.

Sam, a small business owner with inherited money, was single, very bright, and most engaging. The only child of a distant father and indulgent mother, Sam had grown up as the fat sissy in all his peer groups. Despite his outsider status, he pursued girls with great energy, showering them with inappropriately expensive gifts. His first major depressive episode occurred in adolescence and followed rejection by yet another girl. The pattern of major depressive disorder developing after rejection persisted, and when I first saw him he was in his early 40's and in his fifth episode of major depression. The then available antidepressants prescribed by his internist were of no help.

Our psychotherapy lasted for years during which he had several more major depressive episodes. When not depressed he was seductive in the sense of trying to get me to accept expensive gifts, charming in his approach to my obvious interest in 20th century American novelists, but, on the whole, quite resistant to exploring the underside of his dependent transference.

When in the midst of a major depressive episode he made multiple, intense demands for my attention (wanting daily appointments, 4-6 phone calls a day, etc.) and presented with an overarching hopeless-helpless attitude. In the language of an earlier day, Sam's major depressive disorder was oral in that it centered about dependency and abandonment issues. They provoked in me the sense that nothing I could do would be enough to meet his needs; that, in the absence of an antidepressant response, all I could offer was being and staying where he was which meant dealing with surges of my own sense of helplessness.

Harold's major depression was very different. He, too, was in his 40's when I first saw him and had a history of major depressive episodes going back to his college years. Unlike Sam, however, Harold was married and had two teenage sons. He described a childhood marked by a stern, demanding father who, despite Harold's academic and athletic success, never expressed approval or affection. His relationship with his much less powerful mother provided only some of what was not forthcoming from his father.

Harold's personality structure was rigid and demanding. He had many compulsive traits, relied primarily on black and white thinking, and had considerable difficulty containing his underlying anger. His depressive episodes were always preceded by some real or imaginary failure, following which he would become self-punishing with many feelings of guilt and worthlessness.

Harold's major depressive disorder responded to trycyclic antidepressants. When not in the midst of a major depression, he was affable in a somewhat controlled way, clearly very structured, (reliance on rigid routines and the like), and very bright.

The precipitating experiences leading to his calling me (rather than earlier therapists) involved both his having given up his own accounting practice to manage his wife's trust (becoming, we later decided, a prince consort), and the fact that I had treated with some success a cousin of his.

As with Sam, our psychotherapy lasted for years. Its major focus was on his anger at his father and subsequent identification with him so that he now judged himself as severely as his father had. Thus, the major focus of our work was his self-punitiveness. Just as Sam's depression was oral, Harold's was anal in the sense that it centered about issues of anger, control, and self-loathing.

When depressed Sam and Harold shared many of the symptoms of a major depressive disorder. Each was sad, showed marked decrease in interests, experienced loss of appetite with weight loss, complained of fatigue and insomnia, and reported diminished ability to concentrate. Sam, however, was more preoccupied with suicidal thoughts, and Harold had more intense feelings of worthlessness. There seems no doubt that both fulfilled the criteria for a major depressive disorder with recurrent episodes. And, yet, a case can be made that Sam and Harold have very different disorders. The differences are not only apparent in how they experienced their major depressive disorders, but seem clearly to reflect underlying personality issues. Further, the distinction between these two types of major depression has clear implications for treatment.

Sam and Harold's different types of major depressive disorders brings to mind the absence of such distinctions in contemporary clinical thinking, including diagnostic considerations. That the two different types of major depression are not based only on "soft" clinical impressions is illustrated by the work of Blatt and his colleagues (1). Blatt, a psychologist—psychoanalyst at Yale, along with his colleagues, have reported for 30 years on an extensive series of clinical studies and research on these two types of depression. He calls them "anaclitic" (dependent) and "introjective" (self-punitive). They are personality configurations that are differentially sensitive to different kinds of life events leading to depression. Blatt developed the Depression Experiences Questionnaire (DEQ) that identified these two different interactions between personality and the distinctive quality of the experienced depression. Scores of studies have compared the DEQ findings with other psychological measures, and longitudinal prospective studies demonstrate that both the anaclitic and the introjective configurations predict the severity of future depressive disorders.

Blatt's work began with his clinical experiences and the psychoanalytic theory that guided them, moved to the development of a reliable measuring instrument, and explored the predictable relationships between his instrument and others used in the study of depression, all of which led to longitudinal, prospective studies. Taken as a whole, Blatt's contribution is an outstanding example of testing psychoanalytic premises in a systematic way. Further, the delineation of two different personality configurations, with differing sensitivities to environmental events and two resulting forms of depression appear to have clear implications for treatment. Patients, for example, with the anaclitic type of depression seem to do much better with more supportive psychotherapies, and those with the introjective type fare better with less supportive psychoanalytic therapies.

There are not, to my knowledge, any systematic studies of the effectiveness of various antidepressants in these two psychodynamically different forms of major depression. It would also be interesting to know, for example, if Caspi and his colleagues would have found that the 5-HTT polymorph influencing depression through impacting responses to life stress would have been equally influential in the anaclitic and introjective types of depression (2).

In reviewing Blatt's work the issue of what accounts for which research becomes incorporated into the current mainstream of clinical therapy and practice becomes obvious. Although I suspect that many factors operate in concert, it is hard for this clinician not to conclude that it is because his work has its roots in psychoanalysis and does not readily fit in a disease model of psychiatric disorders.

This I find most unfortunate. If psychiatry is to be truly inclusive, its model of psychopathology needs to attend as diverse a group of variables as possible. If the ticket for inclusion is a strong empirical foundation, Blatt's work clearly qualifies.

References

1. Blatt, S.J. (2004). *Experiences of Depression: theoretical, clinical, and research perspectives.* Washington, D.C.: American Psychological Association.
2. Caspi, A., Sugden, K. Moffitt, T.E., et al (2003). "Influence of Life Stress on Depression: Moderation by a Polymorphism in the 5 – HTT Gene," Science, 301:18, July, 386-389.

January 2006

16

RESPECTING RIGIDITY?

At 15 she was hospitalized because her behavior had been out of control for over a year. Angry and defiant, she refused to go to school, was aggressively promiscuous, and had been arrested several times for shoplifting. Three weeks of inpatient studies resulted in a provisional diagnosis of borderline syndrome. Her parents, members of a fundamentalist church, refused to comply with staff recommendations for longer hospitalization, removed her against medical advice, and took her to a church-run rural residential center where she remained for several years. The residential center provided a strict, rule-oriented environment with an emphasis on bible study and work.

Twenty-five years later she was married and the mother of two children. Her life centered about her fundamentalist church, a strict right and wrong code of behavior, and profound convictions about the correctness of her rule-oriented life. She believed that her adolescent behavior had resulted from the devil's influence and that her several years at the religious residential center had saved her life by ridding her of the devil.

This lady's transformation from a chaotic adolescent to a rigid adult can be understood from different perspectives, but here I wish to focus on it as an often overlooked example of psychological growth. The thesis is that systems (including personality) move from chaos to rigidity to flexibility. A rigid system - however constricted - is more adaptive than a chaotic one. Further, a system cannot change directly from chaos to flexibility: there is always an intermediate and rigid intervening structure. Whoever heard, for example, of a government moving directly out of anarchy to democracy? History teaches us that anarchy is invariably followed by totalitarianism. Democracy may or may not then develop.

The important issue is whether the system becomes fixated at the rigid level of organization or goes on to develop a more flexible structure. We are developing greater understanding of the multiple ways in which some adults move from rigidity to greater flexibility, but it is clear that many do not.

The 40 year-old woman described in the opening clinical vignette appears fixated at a rigid level of personality organization. Whether, in the years to come, she will move in the direction of greater flexibility is impossible to know. If she does not, however, it is important to recognize that her adult rigidity is more adaptive than her adolescent chaos.

Psychotherapists have their reasons for questioning the relative adaptiveness of rigid personality structures. Such person's ego mechanisms are usually immature: humor, anticipation, altruism and other mature defenses are absent. Their cognitive style involves limited self-reflection, absolutism, and the inability to sustain paradox and doubt. Relationship patterns show little capacity for intimacy and often emphasize power and control. There is little reason for clinicians to think of adaptiveness when involved with such persons.

In addition, clinicians most often see such persons as patients when their rigid personalities hove failed to protect them from developmental challenges or external stress. They present with symptoms of acute psychosis or major depression and when such symptoms are alleviated by medication, the clinician is often unable to reach beyond the denial and concreteness, "You have a chemical disorder," is a convenient way of giving up the attempt to make contact (The fact that all psychopathology involves chemical disorders does not explain with whom and why the clinician makes such pronouncements nor the clinical circumstances in which the patient's best interests are served).

The movement back and forth between rigidity and chaos is illustrated in the 20 years I treated a young man who presented initially in the midst of an acute psychosis. He experienced threatening auditory hallucinations, retreat from social relationships, and fragmented, disorganized thinking. With the help of the then-available antipsychotic agents, his symptoms gradually disappeared, to be replaced, however, by a severe obsessional state. His obsessional thoughts invaded most waking moments and were relieved only by self-medication with large amounts of alcohol. He functioned at this rigid level for several years, only occasionally and for short durations able to hold down a warehouse job. Then, without any detectable precipitating experience, he suddenly once again became psychotic. This time, however, his psychosis was a classical manic state. He became hyperactive, over-talkative, and grandiose. Once again his symptoms were brought under control by appropriate medication, and he returned to a severe obsessional level of functioning. Throughout my lengthy involvement with him there were multiple switches from psychosis to obsessionalism and back to psychosis. My attempts at supportive psychotherapy did not seem to influence his clinical course despite his faithfulness in coming and clear expressions of faith in my competence. Although significantly incapacitated by his obsessional thoughts, he functioned better at this rigid level of organization than when chaotically psychotic.

As I review this long clinical experience it is easy to ask myself if it might have been in his best interests if he had been offered a "chemical disorder' formulation after several years of psychotherapy. I was concerned, however, about the impact of that formulation on his hope to get well enough to return to college. It was a sticky dilemma for me, however clear the answer might seem in retrospect.

One does see persons with rigid personalities who have not decompensated in couples and family therapy. Almost invariably the spouse or other family member is the identified patient. In such contexts the rigid person's lack of empathy, negative affects, and controlling mechanisms are obvious. What is sometimes uncovered is such persons' underlying fears of being overwhelmed either from within or without with resulting chaos.

A couple seen in marital therapy illustrates this type of rigidity. They were middle-aged, she a housewife and he a successful professional. She had a treatment resistant major depression, and they were referred by her therapist because of the ineffectiveness of psychotherapy and multiple antidepressants. In the initial couples interview, he was angry, controlling, and clearly contemptuous of her. He interrupted her constantly, dismissed her occasional attempts to express her feelings and thoughts, and verbalized directly his disbelief in "all this psychobabble." All she had to do was make up her mind to forget her symptoms.

He came from an impoverished background and achieved economic success through hard work and imposing a rigid structure to his life. My initial and tentative formulation involved, in part, his struggle to both avoid being overwhelmed both by his repressed pain and rage and his belief in a dangerous world. Her depression threatened his sense of control and brought him close to consciously experiencing helplessness and the loss of his rigid defenses.

A third problem making some such persons difficult for clinicians is the often vast differences in the value orientations of patient and therapist. At a personal level, I find that most such persons have a much more conservative life philosophy than I do. They are not the type of person I have established long-term, intimate friendships with. I have to struggle to keep those differences from interfering with the development of a therapeutic alliance. In that struggle understanding that a rigid system is both more adaptive than a chaotic one and can be understood as a defense against the fear of chaos is often helpful.

September 2003

17

LOSING YOUR SPIT

He was in his early 60s and a master carpenter who had helped build our house in the east Texas piney woods some 20 years ago. I asked him abut his cousin who had helped him with the house, and he paused then said sadly, "Doc, he just lost his spit." When I cocked my head, he went on, "You know, he just stopped trying to be in charge of his life—his work, family, and even his health. Just sort of gave up."

The piney woods of east Texas occupy—or once did—the eastern third of the state and were part of the same great forest that spread from the eastern coast of the Atlantic ocean. This mostly rural area retained southern values, and a staunch individualism prevailed. Losing one's spit in this country was a turning away from this important value.

I do not know what the cousin's circumstances really were. Depression, alcohol abuse, and other syndromes come quickly to mind. The intent of this essay, however, is not to explore the cousin's predicament: rather it is to explore some of the implications of believing that one is in control of one's life and then losing it or in the words of my informant, having and losing your spit.

As I write my thoughts turn to two persons who appear to fall at extreme points on a continuum of self-control. One is a man I saw in couples therapy. Although he grew up poor in a family dominated by his father's severe alcoholism he recalls himself as a very driven child. "I always had goals and nothing deterred me from them," he noted with clear pride. "Being in control has always been very important to me and is responsible for my success." When I first saw him he seemed unaware that his emphasis on control played an important role in his wife's unhappy retreat from him.

Contrast this patient with a fictional middle-aged man, Joe Allston, from Wallace Stegner's novel, The Spectator Bird (1).

"As for Joe Allston, he had been a wisecracking fellow traveler in the lives of other people, and a tourist in his own. There had not been one significant event in his life that he had planned. He has gone downstream like a stick getting hung up in eddies and getting flushed out again, only half understanding what he floated past, and understanding less with every year. He knows nothing that posterity needs to be told about." (1, p. 7).

Joe Allston's description of himself is totally devoid of anything suggesting a sense of being in control of his life; indeed, he is both a stick floating passively downstream and, hauntingly, a tourist in his own life.

If these two persons are representative of those occupying the extremes of a presumed continuum of self-control, what do we know that accounts for such individual differences? What factors explain how much spit one has?

It is in our attempts to understand the roots of self-control that we immediately run into some problems. The first problem involves the question of how much such a belief is not real but illusory. This introduces the idea of adaptive illusions—that many (if not most) of us share a small group of assumptions that serve the psychological purpose of reducing anxiety, particularly anxiety about randomness (2). One such illusion is the belief that we are much more in control of our lives than we actually are—or that base-rate data indicate. From this perspective we exaggerate to ourselves the extent of control we have over life's direction, and this illusion can, within limits, be adaptive.

The second problem we have with the concept of self-control is that it is so connected to or overlaps with so many other important personality characteristics that it is difficult to sort out. Separateness, autonomy, purpose, planning, order, and power come quickly to mind. Further, and to the extent that it is possible to sort out the distinctiveness of self-control, those factors that influence its development are multiple and undoubtedly interact in complex ways that are beyond our current understanding.

A starting point in mentioning a few of those factors is the role of genetics. Are there combinations of genes that acting in concert establish a level of propensity for subsequent self-control? I would think almost certainly so although specific and documenting twin studies fail to come to mind. In his book on the impact of the present on both the memory of the past and imagination of the future, Gilbert discusses control and writes that we are born with a passion for being in control, our brains are wired for it, we strive for it throughout life because control is so pleasurable, and believing we are in control of our lives—even if the belief is part illusion—is good for our mental health (3).

Then there are the overwhelming data from infant attachment studies demonstrating that a secure attachment to the primary parenting person (a secure base) facilitates the infant's ability to explore his or her world. What also becomes apparent to those of us who see couples is that adults with avoidant attachment patterns often are over-controlling in their close relationships. This appears to be in the service of avoiding the vulnerability that is an inevitable component of psychological closeness. The couples therapy vignette illustrates that what may seem adaptive in work often fails in relationships.

Families also differ in the extent to which they encourage their children to go out into the world and carve their paths, find their passions, or, in other words, be in control of their lives.

There are other perplexing issues. One is the relation of control to health and psychopathology. It seems apparent that those with unusually strong compulsive features with their emphases on control are particularly apt to struggle with rigidity and relationship problems. Indeed, at certain levels it is possible to understand extreme self-control as part of the effort to avoid closeness.

At the other end of the continuum Joe Allston demonstrates that there are persons who believe they have had little control over the direction of their lives. Thus, it appears that like many other personality characteristics a healthy or adaptive level of self-control involves the midrange, neither too much nor too little.

Despite all the complexities and unknowns about self-control, what can be said about losing one's spit? I believe the most important answer is for the clinician to not jump to conclusions; rather to approach each patient with as open an attitude as possible. In the present climate of categorical thinking the first consideration may be of some sort of depressive disorder. Others will explore whether losing one's spit is more a reflection of developmental processes such as the midlife tasks of reappraisal of one's life dream and the beginning of a more generative stance toward the world.

Although there are other theoretical lenses through which the clinician might view losing one's spit, it seems important to acknowledge that such a loss may be for the better or worse. The man seen in marital therapy needed to lose some of his spit if he hoped to save his marriage. Joe Allston seems to believe that he never had any, and, if so, the clinician's task is to explore whether Joe really wants to try to find some.

There is much more that can be said about losing one's spit, but for present purposes it is perhaps enough to acknowledge that the concept is an intriguing one, and that we have much to learn.

References

1. Stegner, W. (1976). *The Spectator Bird.* New York: Penguin Books.
2. Taylor, S.E., Brown, J.D. (1988). "Illusion and Well-being: A Social Psychological Perspective on Mental Health". Psychological Bulletin, 103(2):193-210.
3. Gilbert, D. (2007). *Stumbling on Happiness.* New York: Vintage Books.

June 2008

18

BRAIN DISEASE AS POLITICAL METAPHOR

At the end of her brief presentation I asked the medical student what the patient, a middle-aged and chronically depressed man, thought about his depression—about its causes and the factors that influenced its remissions and relapses.

"He believes he has a brain disease," the medical student responded.

"How do you think he came to such a conclusion?" I asked.

"I don't know," she said, "but would bet he has been told that such was so by those who see him in the outpatient clinic."

"Why would they tell him that?" I asked.

"Well," she said, "again, I don't know, but I think it's common to tell patients they have a brain disease in the hope they'll take their meds."

"What do you think? Is it helpful to you to think that depression and other psychiatric disorders are brain diseases?"

"I really don't know. A lot of what we heard in our lectures was about neurotransmitters and all of that, but I still don't have a clear idea of what psychiatry is all about," she said, with what seemed both interest and confusion.

If one lives long enough it is possible to experience psychiatry's sequential bandwagons of reductionism. I started my training as the old "organic" psychiatry with its electroshock and insulin coma was being replaced by psychoanalysis. The exciting idea that all or most of all of human woe stemmed from intrapsychic conflict, and that the truth (accurate interpretations) could set one free was as patently reductionistic as are all prior and subsequent simplistic causal schemes. I also recall the interpersonal bandwagon with its "relationships drive one mad" reductionism, and how carefully my board examiners in 1958 explored my knowledge of the "double bind."

The current bandwagon of reductionism is the brain disease metaphor. Psychiatric syndromes—particularly those of the major type—are all simply the outcome of genetic influences on the neurotransmitter ballet in the synaptic cleft. Developmental experiences and current contextual influences are, at best, epiphenomena. The brain disease metaphor is dependent upon a nosology of descriptive diagnoses emphasizing clear distinctions between types, and, in order to deal with the many patients whose dilemmas fall through the cracks, an ever increasing number of types must be elaborated.

The brain disease metaphor overlooks recent neuroscientific findings calling attention to the inseparability of brain and experience. Quantitative behavioral genetic findings indicate that all or most all personality traits have genetic loading. Thus, how the environment responds to the individual is determined partially by the individual's genetic makeup. There is no environmental response entirely free of genetic influence. The environment, however, also influences genetic activity. It does so by turning on and off genetic activity. Although much of the research in this intriguing area involves the motor cortex (as, for example, string players having larger cortical representations of fingers on the left hand than on the nonstring playing right hand), there is also evidence that stress over time increases circulating stress hormones, reduces hippocampal volume, and is associated with memory loss. Since much of stress is interpersonal, such findings lend support to Sapolosky's statement, "the behavior of one human can change the pattern of genetic activity in another" (1, p. 44).

Stress is, however, a slippery concept, and we are a long way from understanding the kinds of relationship processes that may alter genetic activity. If I had to guess I would think first about those processes that result in prolonged and profound feelings of hopelessness and/or helplessness, for those affects are so often involved in the narrative turning points along the road to severe psychopathology.

At any rate, it seems increasingly likely that genetic activity is not entirely free from environmental influences. Thus, thinking in terms of either environment or brain is a misleading reductionism. Describing major depression, for example, as a brain disease is true only to the same extent as being moved by a sunset or piece of Brahms can be usefully described in terms of synaptic activity. Major depression, sunsets, and Brahms are, of course, the result of brain activity, but stating that such is so has little explanatory value, and, further, minimizes or excludes the importance of individual and contextual differences.

Thus, from the perspective of these intriguing neuroscientific findings, the brain disease metaphor is scientifically misleading. If repeated enough it can come to be considered as literally true. Trainees can come to believe its validity and, as a result, may fail to explore the complex interaction of genetic propensities, narrative identity, and the development and function of symptoms. It taps into what Stephen Jay Gould has called our ingrained tendency to think dichotomously (2). What, then, are the advantages of using the brain disease metaphor?

First, it appears to have remarkable political power in that it is a rallying cry for equal insurance coverage of mental health benefits. If after all, major depression is much like diabetes—only the organ is different—why should insurance coverage be denied for brain disease? Although the battle for parity is only in its early stages, the brain disease metaphor has brought new vigor to advocacy groups and encouraged the participation of influential political leaders.

Second, the brain disease metaphor can lead to the reduction or alleviation of guilt in family members of psychiatric patients. The "We must have done something wrong" perspective is deeply rooted in our culture but also received unfortunate support by reductionistic proponents of the earlier psychoanalytic and family therapy bandwagons.

Third, the brain disease metaphor can stimulate research interest (and funding) into the complex inseparability of brain and experience in the so often chronically disabling major psychiatric syndromes.

So, at the very least, we are presented with a conundrum. A metaphor that seriously distorts the complexity of human existence has considerable social utility. For me the dilemma is not easily resolved. Until, that is, I think of the many other metaphors I have endorsed because of their utility without believing them to be true. Years ago during the psychoanalytic bandwagon, for example, we accepted without much serious thought the idea that depression was "anger turned inward." This now embarrassing reductionism did have a limited utility as a metaphor in that it encouraged clinicians to explore the relationship matrix in which depressive symptoms flourished. I need to keep such earlier reductionisms in mind when I chafe as colleagues speak of depression or schizophrenia as simply brain diseases.

References

1. Sapolsky, R. (1997). "A Gene For Nothing." Discover, October
2. Gould, S.J. (2000). "How The Vulva Stone Became a Brachioprad" in *The Lying Stones of Marrakech.* New York: Three Rivers Press

July 2002

Part II

On Relationships With Others

19

ARE THERE GENERAL LAWS OF RELATIONSHIPS?

There is much evidence of the importance of a central relationship in determining the quality of a person's life. The nature of the relationship, for example, is reciprocally related to individual psychological health, life satisfaction, and overall happiness. Despite this importance, there is disagreement among professionals about even the most basic properties of relationships.

One such issue is whether there are general laws of relationships; that is, for example, do all couples entering a relationship with a hoped-for indefinite future have to deal with the same issues, issues that are intrinsic to the process of relationship formation?

Resistance to the premise of general laws of relationships may reside in part in the belief that each relationship is unique, even special, and the idea of general laws of relationships implies a sameness that detracts from a particular relationship's specialness.

Therapists who treat couples need to be clear in their own minds about the operation of general laws of relationships. I believe there are such laws and that understanding them provides a helpful theoretical base from which to treat couples. A much simplified clinical vignette may help to illustrate this position.

Harry and Sally, both physicians, came to see me after six years of marriage because of continuing conflict. Sally defined the problem as Harry's remoteness and workaholism. In turn, Harry focused on Sally's neediness and anger. Both of them described difficult childhoods in dysfunctional families and failed adult relationships. In the office they were both angry, argued about the truth, interrupted each other frequently, and used the language of undesirable personality traits in their intense blaming each other.

After mostly observing their interaction for 20 minutes, I stopped them and told them that I had seen enough of their interaction to get some sense of what was going on and now wished to begin to get information on both their individual lives and a clearer view of the development of their relationship.

Why did I take charge of the interview after 20 minutes of observing? What had I observed, and how had I interpreted what I observed? Here is where theory enters the picture.

The premise that two basic individual motivational systems involve the needs for both separateness and connectedness finds acceptance in a wide variety of theories of individual psychology. Whether called agency and communion, approach-avoidance, attachment and separation—individuation, or I-Thou this dialectic is considered as a basic motivational force. It is thought that heredity, early attachment experiences, family "rules", and other experiences in concert result in an adult's balance of separateness and connectedness. When two persons begin to construct a relationship, differences in their balances may become apparent as the idealizations and mergers of the endorphin phase begins to fade. Each partner then attempts to impose on the relationship his or her need for a particular balance. What may result is a clash of wills, a power struggle, the goal of which is to control the definition of the relationship. The struggle involves not only the physical dimensions of separateness and connectedness but also agreeing or disagreeing about important issues, values, and commitments. Being of "one mind" is an (perhaps, the) important form of closeness. Thus, a general law of relationships is that the issue of separateness and connectedness must be confronted by couples seeking a long-lasting relationship.

A second general law of relationships flows from the first. It is not possible to have a lasting relationship without dealing with the issue of power. Power, as used here, translates as the attempt to influence the other. When there are clear differences in the preferred balance of separateness and connectedness each partner will use those power mechanisms that characterize his or her level of psychological maturity. These range from infantile tantrums to emphatic imperatives to negotiation.

A third general law of relationships is that there are but a handful of relationships structures resulting from the need to deal with the balance of separateness and connectedness that is to prevail in the relationship. If the partners have much the same needs for both separateness and connectedness, the relationship is apt to go smoothly. Partners with strong needs for separateness, for example, may find great satisfaction in a relationship that others would find lacking closeness. Another usually smooth relationship comes about when partners have only moderate differences in their balances, and each brings to the relationship considerable ability to negotiate differences.

Another resulting relationship structure is dominance and submission. One partner has more power in defining the relationship and imposes his or her balance of separateness and connectedness on the less powerful partner. Many of these relationships work moderately well if the power imbalance suits both partner's needs and if the balance of separateness and connectedness is thus acceptable to both. It is not, however, a relationship structure that facilitates the continuing psychological maturation of either partner. Dominant-submissive relationships are seen clinically, often when the less powerful partner develops a clinical syndrome—often a depressive disorder or alcohol abuse.

Harry and Sally represent the conflicted outcome of this developmental relationship task. They are unable to agree on the balance, and neither will yield to the other's attempts at imposition. This conflict is so basic that it can invade all aspects of their shared life experiences. The conflict may be more or less always present or may occur episodically, often following experiences of some desired but feared closeness. Indeed, the relationship function of angry conflict may be understood as the production or maintenance of emotional distance.

Although some degree of relationship conflict is inevitable, when the basic structure of the relationship is conflicted there is little to facilitate individual growth. It is surprising that some basically conflicted relationships last a lifetime. One explanation is that it provides a predictable (if unhappy) way to go through life. Predictability is purchased at the expense of closeness.

Although there are other types of relationship structures growing out of the need to find an acceptable balance of separateness and connectedness, the intent here is not a complete exposition, rather to illustrate the role of a theory involving general laws of relationships as a guide to couples therapy. There are, of course, other laws that could be discussed, but for that the reader is referred elsewhere (1). What I wish to emphasize here are the clinical advantages of a theory-driven therapy based on the idea that there are general laws of relationships.

The primary advantage is that such an understanding gives the therapist a perspective enabling him or her to make sense of what often presents as chaotic material. To move beyond the often confusing specifics of a couple's presentation to an initial understanding of the developmental processes of relationship formation may result in the therapist's ability to intervene at a more helpful level.

At the same time such an approach can facilitate the couple's focus of attention away from blaming each other to one that centers on what is going on between them. If the problem is understood as resulting from the partner's personality characteristics, one is relatively powerless to change the relationship, but to understand that the problem is interactional, that a partner's behavior is responsive to one's own behavior, is empowering.

Although there are other advantages to the belief that there are general laws of relationships and to base one's therapy on such a belief, is it best before ending this essay to emphasize again that not all experts agree on this approach. These clinicians would argue that such an approach is not truly egalitarian—rather a so-called expert-dummy approach in which the clinician presumes that he or she knows what works best in relationships. These clinicians would likely suggest that such a theoretical perspective is primarily in the service of assuaging the therapist's anxiety about a genuine encounter and avoids dealing with each couple's uniqueness.

Those who challenge the idea of general laws of relationships often raise important issues like those noted. How is the therapist to know that following a particular theory may be in the service of avoidance of encounter and uniqueness? What are the tradeoffs involved in theories that emphasize encounter and uniqueness? At the heart of the matter is the complex issue of how the therapist uses (or tries to) his or her power. Can, for example, one's work be guided by the premise of general laws of relationships and still strive for collaborative relationships with patients? Do firmly embedded interactional patterns such as those quickly demonstrated by Harry and Sally require powerful interventions? If so, should the power be open and direct as in "stop that" or subtle and indirect as in "what a distressing conversation?"

Although these questions only begin to hint at what we have yet to learn about the crucial processes of all sorts of therapies, it is also important to keep in mind that in clinical work the principal mandate is to be helpful. Thus, the test of any theory is more utility than truth.

References

1. Lewis, J.M. (1997). *Marriage As a Search for Healing: Theory, Assessment, and Therapy*. New York: Brunner-Mazel.

January 2005

20

ADULT EXPERIENCES, GENETIC ACTIVITY, AND MATURATION

Why is it that experiencing a new love relationship or coping with a severe crisis have such different outcomes for different persons? For some the new relationship or crisis is a positive turning point and the apparent impetus for psychological maturation. For others, however, the result is not positive—rather their adjustment patterns remain dysfunctional or worsen.

The assumption that has dominated clinical thinking above this question is that the answer involves pre-existing personality strengths. It is those fortunate persons who are most apt to profit from new relationships or coping with adversity. That assumption has not been systematically validated, and recent developments concerning the role of gene-environment interactions in psychopathology offer another way of looking at the different outcome experienced by different persons encountering the same or similar life experiences. It is, perhaps, in the genes. The premise would be that the multiple genes involved in personality characteristics like autonomy and relational ability are turned on in some but not all persons by certain life experiences. First, though, where do we learn about the life experiences?

The most obvious source for such leads are careful longitudinal studies that, using state-of-the-art measurements, follow persons from early childhood well into adulthood. Even the most accomplished of these studies, however, have, at best, only measures of the amount of variance due to genetic factors (1). We simply do not know which genes (combinations of such) play their roles in important developmental propensities like autonomy and relatedness. Thus, in assuming the gene-environment interactional perspective we infer that certain experiences turn on or off the as yet unknown genes that produce the proteins that influence the brain circuits involved in such maturational outcomes.

The same dilemma holds for the second source of clues about adult experiences that reverse or modify the adult consequences of childhood trauma; the autobiographical narratives of nonclinical subjects. During the last fifty years I have had the opportunity to be involved with over 800 nonclinical subjects in exploratory interviews. These persons were applicants for a residency training program, research volunteers for studies exploring family health and dysfunction, and, more recently, aspirants for the priesthood or diaconate in the Episcopal Church. The total interview time ranged from one to four hours, and, the interviews had several objectives. One was essentially categorical: Did the subject describe symptoms that, grouped together, are considered descriptive of psychiatric syndromes? The other objective, more pertinent to the concerns of this essay, involved the development of subjects' autobiographical stories, their coherence, underlying themes, turning points, and other identifying characteristics.

There are but a handful of adult experiences of these nonclinical subjects that are described as major life turning points that appear to undo or modify the psychological consequences of childhood trauma. The most common of such experiences is a new relationship with a loving other. These new relationships often follow years of unsuccessful relationships many of which appear to have been of the same pattern as the original painful childhood relationships. Although we do not know how they happen to occur, the new relationships are described in ways that suggest the characteristics of well-functioning marriages in the research accomplished over many years at the Timberlawn Research Foundation (See, for example, 2). The relationship structure is clear, affection openly expressed, and power (particularly in defining the relationship) is mostly shared. There is a high level of commitment to the relationship, joint problem-solving is well developed, and psychological intimacy (the sharing of vulnerabilities) is often present. In such a relationship partners develop an increased ability to function with autonomy and to feel a new-found safety in closeness. As a consequence they appear to have matured psychologically.

Many of these nonclinical subjects with dysfunctional families of origin and prior relationship failures ascribe their new and positive experiences to their partners' characteristics. "He (or she) is so loving, stable, and sensitive that I finally grew in my ability to trust, express myself, and change old, destructive behaviors" was said in different ways by these subjects. What is not known, however, is how such healing relationships come to be. Although luck may play a role, there are likely other factors that influence how a person with traumatic childhood experiences and adult relationship failures finally selects a different type of partner and co-constructs a transforming relationship.

Although a new romantic relationship (usually marital) was the most common, other relationships with psychotherapists, close friends, ministers, and important others were also described. The shared characteristics in all of these "healing" relationships included emotional intensity, reciprocity (in the sense that the relationship was seen as important to both participants), and sufficient time—usually several years.

It is also apparent that deeply spiritual experiences can also be associated with evidence of personal growth. These are usually gradual and are described often as a new and more intense relationship with a loving God.

Another type of adult experience that appeared to promote psychological growth involved the resolution of a severe crisis. Many of the crises fit the description of major depression; a small number involved alcohol abuse; but a substantial minority did not fit any syndromal pattern. Many of the subjects describing the crisis pattern received psychiatric care (psychotherapy most often, but psychotropic drugs also). There remains some debate about what has been called the post-traumatic growth syndrome. Some students believe that the reported growth is real and others emphasize that believing one has been positively changed by struggling with adversity is but a part of coping with that adversity and does not necessarily reflect objectifiable psychological growth. I have discussed this intriguing issue in an earlier column (3).

Changes in systems of meaning was the most common change mechanism described for the entire group by those who appeared to mature as the result of resolution of crises. Almost all of these subjects described a movement away from self-interests (e.g. accomplishments) to the search for meaning in relationships with others (e.g. generativity).

A small number of these nonclinical subjects did not describe either a new and healing relationship or the resolution of a serious crisis. Rather, they found it difficult to account for their maturation. "I guess I finally grew up" was said in one way or another by these subjects.

The current thinking about adult maturation is almost exclusively psychological. Psychoanalytic theory emphasizes the internalization of important others and the replacement of earlier internal object representations with new and more positive ones. Attachment theory describes changes in internal working models of relationships brought about by new and secure adult attachments that replace or modify insecure attachment styles learned in childhood. Cognitive theory emphasizes much the same processes that result in revised internal relationship schemata.

Although there is growing appreciation that sustained behavioral changes must involve synaptogenesis and changed brain circuitry, there has been little attention paid to how the types of experiences described in this essay may operate through their impact on the genetic activity required for those brain changes. It seems reasonable to speculate that as the genes influencing the propensity for complex traits like autonomy and relatedness are identified we will be able to better understand why the same adult experiences that appear to facilitate growth in some fail to do so for others. It may well turn out that, as has been demonstrated for certain forms of psychopathology, healthy adult development may require both certain types of experiences and the presence of certain combinations of genes.

References

1. Reiss, D., Plomin, R., Neiderhiser, J.M., Hetherington, E.M. (2000). *The Relationship Code: Deciphering Genetic and Social Influences on Adolescent Development.* Cambridge, Mass: The Harvard University Press.
2. Lewis, J.M. (1997). *Marriage as a Search for Healing: Theory, Assessment and Therapy.* New York: Bernel Books.
3. Lewis, J.M. (2007). "The Post-Traumatic Growth Syndrome: Fact or Fiction?" December, Psychiatric Times. Reprinted in *Reflections: On Relationships With Self and Others,* 2009.

April 2008

21

AND NOW, YOUR PARENTS' RELATIONSHIP?

She paused for a few moments and then responded, "I don't know when children may begin to think their parents are unhappy with each other except, of course, if there are a lot of arguments and fights. My parents didn't argue or fight, but they were not openly affectionate either. They were just there, and I never thought about it—nor did I have any other marriages to compare, no grandparents or aunts and uncles around. Then, when I was 12 or 13 my mother began talking to me about how unhappy she was with my father. She told me he was cold, uncaring, and, at times mean. I remember feeling very uncomfortable, like I was being asked to take sides."

These recollections of a parental marriage were shared with me in one of several exploratory interviews that is a part of the ordination process for the Episcopal Church. The primary intent of the interviews is to screen out aspirants for whom a religious vocation may be psychologically unsuitable. One module of the data I seek is the pattern of interpersonal relationships across the aspirant's life. Most of these persons are in midlife, and it is often possible to identify a clear pattern of relationships beginning with early attachment experiences with both parents. Another source of helpful data is the nature of the recalled parental relationship, the adult relationship most persons' early development is immersed in and reactive to.

In contrast to the thousands of studies of infant and adult attachment patterns, there has been little systematic research on the developmental impact of various parental relationship patterns. Our own research at the Timberlawn Research Foundation has demonstrated that observed parental interactions influence the child's early development independent of the child's relationship with each parent (1). The problem, however, with adult recollections of early life parental relationships is they often change over time and may do so outside the person's awareness. One longitudinal study, for example, reported major changes in the recall of the parental warmth from adolescence to midlife (2). Another of our own studies revealed that family or origin memories of new mothers changed in response to the availability and helpfulness of their husbands (3). These findings are part of a growing number that suggest that just as past influences present, the present influences how the past is recalled.

The Episcopal aspirant's recollections of her childhood experience of her parents' marriage are not, I believe, unusual. Unless there is obvious discord or clear revelation of marital unhappiness, the child denies to himself or herself that there is anything wrong. It is simply too threatening to believe that one's world may fall apart. Those readers who are inclined to skepticism about childhood denial need to be aware of studies that document the relationship of parental marital unhappiness to physiologic markers of anxiety in children as young as four (4). It seems clear from such studies that an unhappy parental marriage is apt to result in anxiety for at least some of their children. We are not, however, able to say which children are most vulnerable. Can age, gender, sibling rank-order or other relatively straight-forward variables be crucial? Or is vulnerability a much more complex process involving, for example, the child's affect sensitivity, anxiety level, or early identifications? We simply do not know what factors influence whether a child may be particularly susceptible to what is going on in his or her parents' relationship.

We also are ignorant of whether it is simply the lack of parental marital satisfaction that is toxic to some children or whether specific parental relationship patterns are—separate and apart from level of satisfaction—disruptive to vulnerable children's development. As illustrations, two very different relationship patterns can be described. One can be called a dominant-submissive, complimentary relationship: the other a distant but nonconflicted pattern. The first is illustrated by the reflections of a candidate for a psychiatric residency. He said, "My parents got along well. My father was in charge of everything—money, church, and who checked the locks at night. You might call him a benevolent dictator. He was not harsh—he just took care of everything and the net result was total control. Mother seemed not to mind, seemed even to be very happy with being so well taken care of—it really was sort of a parent-child marriage." He went on to describe his own marriage as one that was very different. "I didn't want all the power—I really wanted a more equal relationship with shared responsibilities, and that's what we have. I'm very happy and think my wife is too."

There are several issues reflected in this vignette. One is the question of how many persons want a marriage like that of their parents? One study of spouses with successful marriages reported that only five percent said they based their marriages on that of their parents, but there are no data from representative populations (5). Five percent may be too low: we simply do not know.

A second question is whether dominant-submissive parental marriages that seem acceptable to both parents have any downside for their children? Once again we are without systematic data, but it is not hard to speculate that such marriages may indoctrinate some children with very narrow gender roles. In the example given the risk is that some sons may grow up believing that, like their fathers, they need to be in control of everything, that women are relatively incapable of executive functioning. Daughters are equally likely to grow up with such narrow and reduced expectations of themselves. Exactly what factors may encourage such internalizations and what factors may protect against them are simply not currently known.

Another and very different type of parental relationship is one characterized by the lack of any outward signs of emotional closeness. Such couples often treat each other with civility but their lives seem to be on different tracks. A woman in couple's therapy described her parents' marriage as follows, "They're both really nice persons, but they don't seem very much connected. I've never seen them hold hands, hug, or kiss. They both have friends but not usually the same ones. Their interests are also different—Dad is very literary, surrounded by books, and mother plays golf almost every day. I've often wondered how they came to marry each other and be intimate enough to have two children," she said shaking her head.

Perhaps not surprisingly her complaints about her husband centered about his lack of emotional availability, and initially she did not see the subtle ways in which she discouraged his infrequent attempts to be more available. At one level she had unconsciously selected a partner with whom a crucial aspect of her parents' relationship was re-enacted, not an uncommon repetition. Despite her conscious wish not to repeat this pattern, she had done so, and this speaks to the strength of the early internalization.

It is, then, not just the internalizations of one's relationships with each parent, but the taking into one's developing self the pattern of their relationship that can shape adult life. A recent attempt to study this phenomena has been reported by Story and her colleagues (6). They studied young couples at the time of their marriages and four years later. The partners' initial reports of negativity in their parents' marriages were significant predictors of their own marital outcomes four years later. Both husbands and wives demonstrated observed negative behaviors in their interactions with each other at the four year follow-up. The authors discuss a number of potential mediators of the relationships between reported negativity in the parental marriages and the subsequent development of dysfunctional marital behaviors, but the truth is that we do not know.

It is clear that there is much work to be done to better understand why some persons appear to repeat the often dysfunctional marital patterns of their parents and others do not. We know that the quality of one's marriage is a potent influence on overall life satisfaction, physical and emotional health, and life meaning, so the work to be done has great importance.

References

1. Lewis J.M., (1989). *The Birth of the Family: An Empirical Inquiry.* New York: Brunner-Mazel.
2. Offer D., Katz M., Howard K.I., Bennett E.S., (2000). "The Altering of Reported Experiences." J Am Acad Child Adolesc Psychiatry, 39:6, 735-742.
3. Lewis J.M., Owen M.T., (1996). "Stability and Change in Family-of-Origin Recollections over the First Four Years of Parenthood." Family Process, 34, 455-469.
4. Gottman, J.M., Katz, L.F. (1989). "The Effects of Marital Discord on Young Children's Peer Interaction and Health." Developmental Psychology, 25:373-381.
5. Wallerstein, J.S., Blakeslee, S. (1995). *The Good Marriage: How and Why Love Lasts.* Boston: Houghton Mifflin Co.
6. Story, LB., Karney, B.R., Lawrence, E., Bradbury, T.N. (2004). "Interpersonal Mediations in the Intergenerational Transmission of Marital Dysfunction." Journal of Family Psychology, Vol. 18, No. 3, 519-529.

January 2009

22

THE ENCOUNTER

What's wrong?

I don't feel well.

Do you think you have a bug?

No. It's more that I don't have any energy.

Like exhausted?

Yea. Just woke up feeling this way.

Tell me more about what it feels like.

Kind of sad.

Like you woke up this morning feeling down—sad?

Yea. And I don't know why.

What comes to mind?

Not sure, but I find my father coming to my mind; and he's been dead since I was little.

Like you woke up this morning feeling sad and thinking about your father.

Yea. Everything I missed growing up because he died so young.

You really did miss a lot, and it is sad. It blew your mother away, too.

Yea. There really wasn't anyone there for me for a long time. Maybe until you came along.

And I haven't been so available recently—my promotion and all that.

I know, but I hate to whine.

There is considerable disbelief that such encounters occur outside of psychotherapy. If one asks experienced therapists about how often they and their spouses experience such conversations, the answers range from "rarely" to "occasionally." One colleague, for example, smiled and said, "If such conversations occurred frequently, my wife wouldn't let me leave home." If one asks couples coming for marital therapy, the answer is almost always "never." One woman, for example, said that in 27 years of marriage she and her husband had never spoken to each other in such a way. "I don't think we know how," she added with clear sadness.

We know very little about why such conversations occur in some relationships and not others. We also do not know why they are accorded so much importance when couples with high levels of relationship satisfaction are asked about what contributes to their satisfaction. We are also ignorant of whether and how such encounters facilitate adult psychological maturation.

Perhaps our collective ignorance is understandable. Coontz in writing about the history of marriage, for example, suggests that the belief that marriage should fulfill the emotional needs of spouses is a relatively recent development during the past several hundred years (1). Further, she writes that such a belief contributes to the fragility of marriage by establishing norms that are difficult for many to achieve. Thus, Coontz's historical research indicates that our collective ignorance may reflect in part the recent historical change in beliefs about the basic function of marriage.

The conversations themselves are exploratory in nature. One partner responds to the other's message by attempting to explore what is going on inside the other. Such attempts do not rely on a barrage of focused questions: rather they are more reflective, often responsive to affective cues. Exploratory conversations are characterized by high levels of attention and the absence of advice-giving or judgmental responses. Most of all they reflect a high level of interest in and respect for the other's subjective reality.

Although we know that some couples volunteering for marital-family research demonstrate their capacity for exploratory conversations when, for example, they are asked to discuss differences of opinions, we have no idea of how often this ability is present in representative samples. There is also evidence from the Timberlawn Research Foundation's studies that the individual ego strength of both partners contributes to the ability to have such conversations but ego strength explains only part of the variance (2). This may well reflect a circular interaction: couples with high levels of individual ego strength are more likely to learn to explore each other's subjective reality, and, such explorations may contribute to growth in individual ego strength. Another relevant factor is the concept of emergent relationship qualities; those qualities that emerge from repetitive interactions and are not predictable from individual characteristic. Exploratory conversations are more apt to emerge in the interactions of more mature partners but not from all such couples. Why they emerge in some but not other highly satisfactory relationships is not known.

There are several flourishing ideas about how such conversations may contribute to individual adult maturation. One such idea is the slippery psychoanalytic concept of internalization. We are believed to take into our self-systems the qualities of those we love and who love us in turn. Exploratory conversations may set the stage for internalization by providing the person with an important other who demonstrates interest in and respect for our feelings and ideas. Through internalization we appropriate the other's characteristics into one's relationship with oneself. The interpersonal perspective emphasizes that such conversations enhance the individual's capacity for closeness, trust, and interdependency—thus enhancing individual maturation. Cognitive theory might propose that through such conversations negative working models of self and other are replaced by models that are positive. There are other ideas about how such relationship experiences may facilitate individual maturation, all of which may operate at some level. The truth seems to be, however, that we do not know how relationship experiences translate into individual maturation. Careful longitudinal studies incorporating both interactional and individual characteristics have yet to be done.

There is, however, growing interest in this topic. Siegel, for example, has proposed an interpersonal-neurobiological model of development in which the repetitive experience of such encounters leads to the growth of new synapses in the experience-dependent adult brain (3). Sapolsky has written about how some (mostly stressful) interpersonal experiences may turn on or off the genes necessary for proteins involved in neurotransmitter metabolism (4). Although not describing encounter experiences he proposes that interpersonal relationships can influence genetic activity. Kielcolt-Glasser and her colleagues have demonstrated the distinctive impact of both rapport and conflict on the participants' cellular immune functioning (5). Thus, from very different perspectives the interface between interpersonal relationships and brain structure and functioning is attracting needed theoretical and research attention.

Of course, creative writers have been well ahead of us in emphasizing the positive impact of relationships on individual adult maturation. Carol Shields wrote that "life is an endless recruitment of witnesses", and surely she spoke to the universal need to have our inner experience noted, respected, and validated (6). Toni Morrison described why Sixto walked 30 miles each way to visit his girlfriend (7). It was because she was "a friend of the mind" —a person who helps one know better one's own feelings and thoughts. The poet, Stanley Kunitz, must have also been writing about encounter and knowledge of the self when he wrote"

"Darling, do you remember
the man you married?
Touch me
Remind me who I am" (8, p. 266)

These examples are but a few of many, but they illustrate the point that we need to direct more of our professional energy to understanding just how encounters facilitate adult maturation.

References

1. Coontz, S. (2005). *Marriage, a History: from Obedience to Intimacy or How Love Conquered Marriage*, New York: Viking.
2. Zilbermann, K. (1984). "Ego Development and Patterns of Family Interaction." Dissertation Abstracts International, 45, 1929B.
3. Siegel, D. (1999). *The Developing Mind: Toward a Neurobiology of Interpersonal Experience*, New York: The Guilford Press.
4. Sapolsky, R. (1998). "Is Biology Destiny?" Family Therapy Networker, March/April, pp. 33-35.
5. Kielcolt-Glasser, J. et al (1993). "Negative behavior during marital conflict is associated with immunological down-regulation." Psychosomatic Medicine, 55:5, Sept-Oct, 395-409.
6. Shields, C. (1995). *The Stone Diaries*. New York: Penguin Books.
7. Morrison T. (1988). *Beloved*. New York, Plume Printing.
8. Kunitz, S. "Touch Me" in *The Collected Poems of Stanley Kunitz*, New York: W.W. Norton and Co., 2000.

November 2005

23

RELATIONSHIPS THAT HEAL

Elizabeth had not left her bedroom for six years when, at age 39, her relationship began with her husband-to-be. In the 19 months of their courtship, he visited her 91 times, and they exchanged 573 letters. She was the oldest and favorite of 12 children of a tyrannical father who forbade any of his children to have romantic involvements and who appeared comfortably resigned to a life of dependent invalidness.

In addition to episodes of fever and hemoptysis she experienced insomnia, anorexia, and weakness. Her tubercular symptoms were thus set in the context of depression and were often precipitated by losses. Hysterical symptoms such as the inability to swallow were also present from time to time. Elizabeth was also addicted to the morphine that her physicians prescribed. She had a close, ambivalent relationship with a two-year younger brother, and when he drowned as a young adult she experienced what sounds like a three-month psychosis. Despite her many symptoms and comfortable acceptance of the role of the invalid, she lived through her writing and became a famous poet with a public image of the caged nightingale.

Robert, six years younger than Elizabeth, was the older of two siblings of a devout, dominating, evangelical mother and a passive father whose position as a bank clerk belied his bookishness and intellectuality. Robert was his parents' favorite and remarkably indulged. Nothing was required of him: he was to spend his life studying whatever he wished, and, despite the family's limited economic resources, there was no pressure on him to work and help support the family. Indeed, save for his own writing, he never worked a day in his life. Robert was also very dependent on his mother and could not, for example, fall asleep unless he had kissed her goodnight. This dependent behavior continued until he married.

He was something of a social climber and sought out older women who idealized him and praised his writing. His writing, noted to contain many morbid themes , did not find public or critical acceptance.

Robert can be understood as both dependent and narcissistic. Beneath the surface he struggled with anger, which his writing expressed in the themes of evil, torture, and death.

Thus, Robert and Elizabeth Barrett Browning seemed like unlikely candidates to construct a stable, lasting marriage—let alone one that transformed each of them. And yet they did.

The marriage transformed Elizabeth's life by allowing her to emerge from the dependent relationship with her tyrannical father. It encouraged her to give up a reclusive, invalid status and to engage actively with life. She embraced sexuality and after multiple miscarriages gave birth to a son. She was as active physically (hiking, riding) as her tuberculosis allowed. In short, for the 15 years before her death she produced her best poetry and lived a vigorous, active life without hint of depression.

The marriage also transformed Robert. He was able to escape from his dependent position with his controlling mother and to love a heterosexual partner. Robert's care of Elizabeth was outstanding during those periods when her tuberculosis was symptomatic. He nursed her tenderly through many such periods. Thus, the marriage helped Robert to both grow out of his dependency and temper his narcissism. It was also during these 15 years that he became recognized as a major writer.

The Brownings' marriage is a classical example of the transforming potential of an intense relationship. I suspect that clinicians see relatively few such situations, perhaps because those whose lives have been transformed feel little need for psychotherapy. If one has the opportunity to study nonclinical subjects, however, accounts of such transformations are not rare.

Our understanding of relationships that transform the lives of the participants is in its infancy. We do not know how frequently they occur nor what circumstances facilitate them. Whether there are psychological characteristics of one or both partners that are crucial is likewise not known. We do know, however, some of the descriptive features of such relationships, and it is to these that I next turn.

Our research at the Timberlawn Research Foundation has revealed a small number of relationship characteristics that are present in such marriages (1-3). The first characteristic is that these couples have constructed a relationship in which power is shared. This results in both partners contributing to the definition of their relationship with the result that there is no chronic conflict about whose view of the relationship is to prevail nor does one's partner impose his or her definition on the other. Shared power results in either partner providing leadership as the context demands. The old adage, "Two heads are better than one" is documented by these couples.

Another characteristic of such relationships is respect for subjective reality. Each partner is interested in and respectful of what the other thinks and feels. There is little preoccupation with who is right and who is wrong; rather differences in perceptions, beliefs, and feelings are often the starting points for respectful explorations. As a consequence these differences less often lead to conflicts.

A third characteristic is the capacity to exchange vulnerabilities. These couples usually develop a substantial level of openness with each other about those private feelings, thoughts, hopes, fears, and the like that are associated with feeling vulnerable to criticism, rejection, and other negative responses. It is tempting to link these three descriptive characteristics in a way that suggests that shared power facilitates respect for subjective reality which, in turn, leads to the exchange of vulnerabilities. However logical that sequence appears, we have no data that supports or denies such an orderly progression.

The accounts of the Brownings' marriage indicate that these three characteristics were present (4). They shared power. Each was deferential to the other's wishes, and avoided imposing personal beliefs on the other. Their decisions were almost always made collaboratively.

Robert and Elizabeth were intensely interested in each other's subjective reality and most respectful of their differences. They differed, for example, in their opinions about dueling and the amount and type of discipline to use with their son, but these differences were most often negotiated and rarely led to conflict.

The Brownings were unusually open with each other and shared very private matters both in conversation and their frequent notes to each other.

These descriptive characteristics of shared power, respect for subjective reality, and the exchange of vulnerabilities represent a reasonable starting point in our search to better understand how it is that some relationships transform the lives of the participants, and, as with Elizabeth and Robert, facilitate the emergence from significant psychopathology.

References

1. Lewis J.M. (1989). *The Birth of the Family: An Empirical Inquiry.* New York: Brunner-Mazel.
2. Lewis, J.M. (1997). *Marriage As a Search for Healing: Theory, Assessment, and Therapy,* New York: Brunner-Mazel.
3. Lewis, J.M., Gossett, J.T. (1997) *Disarming the Past: How an Intimate Relationship Can Heal Old Wounds,* Inc. Phoenix, AZ: Zeig, Tucker & Co.
4. The references for the lives of Elizabeth Barrett and Robert Browning are available upon request from the author at P.O. Box 270789, Dallas, Texas 75227.

May 2003

24

REPEAT OR REPAIR?

He came to me at the urging of a friend and initially seemed poised and articulate. This facade faded with his tears as he described the recent ending of a love affair. His partner had left him after two years of living together, and he was depressed, not sleeping, and had lost ten pounds. It did not take long to understand that this painful episode was part of a pattern. He described both of his marriages and his three long-lasting love affairs as ending when the women left him.

In the next several interviews it became apparent that he selected flawed women. All five of his partners were described as narcissistic, dominating, and drug-abusing. In exploring his childhood experiences he described a distant father and a chronically depressed mother. Early in life he became his mother's caretaker, a "good boy" who sought affection and approval from his mother by doing the right thing; that is, taking care of her.

My initial formulation included the idea that his selection of flawed women represented a repetition of his early relationship with his flawed mother. He was drawn to women who needed caretaking. With them, he tried to express his affection by doing the right thing. In turn, he reported that they complained that he was cold and distant in relating to them.

This clinical vignette illustrates the repetition during adult years of a problematic childhood relationship. Contrast it with the following brief report that emphasizes the opposite process, repair of childhood wounds by participating in a healing adult relationship.

He and his wife volunteered through their church for a study of healthy families. The transcripts of his individual interviews and his psychological test data were evaluated as indicating an above average level of psychological health.

His description of his childhood centered about his parents' divorce when he was an infant, the disappearance of his father from his life, and his mother's debilitating rheumatoid arthritis. She was often in considerable pain and spent much of her time in bed. He became her helper and caretaker at an early age.

He met his wife-to-be at the junior college in the neighborhood. He described being attracted to her self-sufficiency, warmth, spontaneity, and humor. They went together for three years before marrying, and, he described her impact upon him in the following way, "She is the most important influence in my life. I was a terribly constricted person, always fearful of making errors. She has helped me get in touch with my deeper feelings, become more expressive, and get over my fears of making mistakes. I owe her more than I can describe."

Most clinicians have little opportunity to hear narratives of repair because they do not, as a rule, interview in depth nonclinical subjects. During the past 40 years, I have heard many such narratives in interviewing over 800 subjects who were applicants for a psychiatric residency program, postulants for the Episcopal priesthood, or research volunteers. One often hears narratives of repair, most frequently involving a healing adult relationship or spiritual experience, and systematic longitudinal research of adult development adds validity to this observation (1).

A number of mechanisms have been proposed in the effort to understand healing relationships. The psychoanalytic concept of internalization —that we take into ourselves the characteristics of those we love—is one. I have described the evidence supporting the idea that the establishment of a strong affective bond and the repair of its inevitable disruptions has been demonstrated in three of the important relationships in which healing or growth occurs (infant-mother, marital, and psychotherapeutic), and, thus, may be considered as the interpersonal context in which internalizations occur (2).

Another perspective on the mechanisms of healing relationships involves the idea of relationships as regulatory systems for the participants. Self-esteem, strong affects, cognitive distortions, defense mechanisms, and physiologic functions such as vascular activity and cellular immune functions may be regulated by transactions between the participants. There is also a body of theory and research called "self-verification theory" that demonstrates that relationships in which one's identity is verified are sought out and valued (3). Thus, even one's basic sense of self can be understood as regulated by interactions with important others.

Internalizations and interpersonal regulatory systems are difficult to study systematically. They are thought to be processes occurring over considerable time spans and outside the awareness of the participants, and appropriate research methodologies are difficult to construct.

As indicated above, there is, at least, considerable thought given to how adult relationships may heal. When it comes, however, to what seems to be a crucial issue—the selection of a partner with whom repeating or repairing a relationship pattern originating in childhood is more likely —we are mired in ignorance. The patient in the first vignette made five choices in which his early relationship with his mother appeared to be repeated. The research subject in the second vignette selected a partner who provided him the opportunity to repair a similar childhood circumstance. What accounts for the difference in these critical choices?

Mate selection is a well-studied phenomenon, and personality, physical characteristics, values, religion, and other more-or-less conscious factors have been identified. The idea that unconscious factors play important roles is widely believed to be true by therapists but is remarkably difficult to demonstrate. One idea is that, in general, persons at the same level of psychological functioning are unconsciously attracted to each other. Another idea is that persons can be attracted to others who are either much like themselves or more-or-less the opposite. Another widely held idea is that it is mostly a matter of luck—one does not really know who the other is until the relationship is well along.

Object relations theory and its derivative, attachment theory, both posit that a central early relationship involving self, other, and the interaction is stored in primitive memory where it functions as an internal object representation, a working model, or going back to Freud, a "stereotype plate." This relationship pattern influences the choice of partner and the nature of the relationship established. Those taking this view emphasize that, although modifications in the pattern can come about as the result of later relationships, there is a strong tendency to repeat the childhood pattern in adult relationships. Thus, this is a transference model of marriage or other important relationships. Research support for such a model has been found in the verbatim transcripts of psychotherapy sessions with outpatients (4). Each patient demonstrated one or several core conflictual relationships. These patterns from childhood also appeared to operate in a central adult relationship and in the emerging transference to the therapist. Although this psychodynamic research and that guided by attachment theory suggest that childhood relationship patterns can be modified by healing adult relationships, they do not shed any light on the question of why some persons repeat and others repair dysfunctional childhood relationship patterns.

This riddle becomes even more complex when the focus is enlarged beyond the processes of selecting a life partner to include the premise that the nature of the evolving relationship is a construction of both partners usually resulting in emergent relationship characteristics that are not completely predictable using each partner's individual characteristics. Thus, the search to understand the processes of repeating and repairing childhood relationship patterns must look beyond the personalities of individuals and their partners to include their interactions with each other. No simple task but, in light of the prevalence of self-reports of healing adult relationships, a worthwhile effort.

References

1. Quinton D., Rutter M., Liddle C. (1984). "Institutional Rearing, Parenting Difficulties and Marital Support", Psychol Med. 14, 107-124.
2. Lewis, J.M. (2000). "Repairing the Bond in Important Relationships: A Dynamic for Personality Maturation", Am J Psych, 157:9, 1375-1378.
3. Swann, W.B., Stein-Seroussi, A., Giesler, P.B. (1992). "Why People Self-Verify", J of Personality and Social Psychology, 62:3, 392-401.
4. Luborsky, L. (1977). "Measuring a Pervasive Psychic Structure in Psychotherapy: The Core Conflictual Relationship Theme" in *Communicative Structures and Psychic Structures*, Ed. Freedman, N., Grand, S., N.Y.: Plenum.

September 2004

25

LOVE AND POWER

There are many who find any connection between love and power unthinkable. Being in love, indeed, has been defined as caring for another without any consideration of power. And yet, many students of loving relationships consider power to be an important factor in determining the course of such relationships. A case vignette may help to illustrate this perspective.

They arrived a few minutes late for their first appointment, and he was clearly angry. "Have trouble finding my office?" I asked. "No," he responded, "She'd be late to her funeral." His contempt was obvious. She was dressed simply, quite obese, and looked depressed, but said nothing.

The initial interview clearly revealed the pattern of their relationship. He did all the talking and when I addressed questions directly to her, he usually interrupted her responses. She averted his gaze but sighed often. He was clearly the dominant spouse, and she behaved like an intimidated child.

The history confirmed the dominant-submissive nature of their relationship. Her major depression and weight gain surfaced several years before our initial contact and followed their youngest child leaving for college. Two years of once-weekly psychotherapy and six different antidepressants had not substantially impacted her symptoms. Her psychiatrist came to believe that the refractory nature of her syndrome was related to the marital situation and asked that I evaluate and treat them with couples therapy if I agreed with that opinion.

He was a poor boy from a rural area whose athletic prowess resulted in a football scholarship to a major state university. There he became a campus hero and met his wife-to-be during his moments of fame. She, in turn, was the favored child of a wealthy, domineering father and passive mother. A beauty queen and fraternity favorite, she was drawn to his self-confidence, physical attractiveness, and campus fame. She became pregnant during their senior year, agreed to the abortion her father insisted upon, and married after graduation when he went to work in her father's business.

She described a marriage in which he was not available emotionally and made all the decisions. In turn, she focused on their three children, the home, and volunteer activities. He described the marriage as "ideal." "I took over the family business, and she was responsible for the home and kids. I think it worked well until our last one left for school," he said.

The problems in trying to be helpful were obvious. First, her depression was severe and had not responded to usual interventions. Second, he was most resistant to considering himself and their relationship as parts of the problem. Third, the helplessness that her symptoms evoked in him was deeply hidden behind his anger and contempt. Fourth, the basic structure of their relationship had been in place for many years. Finally, I would have to struggle to effect alliances with a woman who had found new power in her symptoms and was, at some level, reluctant to give up that power. The problems of alliance-formation with him were also formidable. He was strongly defended, more than usually arrogant, and openly dismissive of psychiatry, psychology, and "all that psychobabble."

My views on the role of power in relationships have been presented in detail elsewhere, and will be summarized only briefly at this time (1). When two persons come together to construct a hopefully enduring relationship, two basic questions must be faced. The first is, "How connected and how separate are we to be?" The second is, "How is the balance of connectedness and separateness to be decided?" It is this second question that opens the door to considerations of power.

If the partners agree on the balance of connectedness and separateness—regardless of the actual balance—relationship formation generally goes smoothly. In the clinical example given the balance was skewed towards separateness and imposed by the more powerful husband. It appears to have been mostly satisfactory to the wife whose life involved the seamless transfer from a dominating father to a dominating husband. Her dependent needs were gratified, but she complained about the lack of emotional closeness. Her needs for closeness were met with her children, and it was only after they all left the house that she became symptomatic. Thus, a balance initially acceptable to both partners may become unacceptable to one or both as different stages of adult development are encountered.

When the partners are confronted with a disagreement about the balance of connectedness and separateness, one of three outcomes occur. As in the clinical example, one partner may impose his or her preferred balance on the other. A second outcome is chronic conflict. Many of the couples appearing for therapy are involved in a struggle in which each partner attempts to impose his or her definition of the relationship on the other. Neither yields and the struggle either goes on and on or leads to the dissolution of the relationship. Some couples restrict the topic of the power struggle to one or several areas (e.g. sex, money, parenting), but for others the conflict invades all areas of life. Other couples present the conflict quite directly. "There is no closeness in our relationship" and "We lead lives that are entirely separate" are not uncommon. One rarely hears the opposite complaint of too much closeness.

There are a large number of empirical studies documenting the deleterious impact on individual physical and psychological health of living in a chronically conflicted relationship. The children of parents with such a relationship are also at increased risk for psychological disturbances.

The third resolution of the need to define the balance of connectedness and separateness is negotiating a balance that is acceptable to both partners. When this negotiated balance involves relatively equal power, the opportunity is realized to construct a relationship that is experienced as highly satisfactory by both partners and provides the psychological climate for healthy development for both the partners and children they may be raising.

How does relatively equal power play a prominent role in the formation of a good relationship? Here the empirical data are scant, and what I describe results from studying the marriages of research volunteers whose marriages meet the criteria of enhanced individual growth and high levels of satisfaction. Equal power increases the likelihood that each spouse will be interested in and respectful of the other partner's thoughts and feelings. Thus, relatively equal power leads to respect for subjective reality. Knowing that there is a good likelihood that one's subjective reality will be respected enhances the probability of increased self-disclosure. Ultimately the self-disclosure may involve thoughts and feelings about which one feels vulnerable. The reciprocal exchange of vulnerabilities is one definition of psychological intimacy, and psychological intimacy is a prominent marker of a good relationship.

As I write this brief outline of how I believe equal power may lead to a growth-facilitating relationship, the result sounds much too linear, much too simple. Certainly it is more complex—all sorts of feedback loops must be involved. Genetic factors influencing approach (connectedness) and avoidance (separateness) must be considered. Sociocultural prescriptions of the ideal balance of connectedness and separateness need consideration. And so the complexity increases. The model so briefly outlined is but a possible skeletal structure.

These considerations of love and power also tap into personal experiences. I grew up in a father-dominated family and internalized a view of marriage in which the man dominated. My mother's underlying sadness and anger about the lack of closeness with my father became obvious to me at an early age. When I married my beautiful, warm, and supportive wife, I had no conscious awareness that underlying these wonderful characteristics was a strong stream of self-determination, stubbornness, and a pervasive opposition to being dominated. Her ways of opposing my usually direct approaches to getting my way were mostly indirect and only occasionally openly oppositional. She softly insisted on an equal voice, and, thankfully, persisted. At length, it became obvious to me that sharing power to define the relationship resulted in both shared responsibility and greater closeness.

So, my interest in the relationship between love and power, as in so many other areas, has both clinical and personal roots. I suspect such is so for many psychotherapists.

Reference

1. Lewis, J.M. (1997). *Marriage As a Search for Healing: Theory, Assessment and Therapy,* New York: Bruner-Mazel.

January 2002

26

WRONG CHOICES

An emphasis in an earlier column was what can be learned from interviewing nonclinical subjects (1). One may hear of life turning points that appear to prompt maturational processes, in particular, alleviation of psychiatric symptoms, greater emphasis on the needs of others, a renewed sense of personal meaning, and enhanced life satisfaction. These turning points are less often reported by patients coming for psychotherapy, and, indeed, one perspective on psychotherapy is that it is a search for change that has not been provided by life experiences. The therapist does not so often hear about healing marriages, growth through adversity, or spiritual experiences in part because psychotherapy is less needed if such healing has already occurred.

What to make of these stories and their turning points remains far from settled. Expert opinions range from those who believe that a person's life story is his or her experienced self or basic identity to others who declare that each of us has multiple life stories, and which story is told is strongly shaped by context (who the story is being told to, their responses, etc.). Regardless of what one makes of life stories, it is hard to deny that the choice of a life partner is usually for better or worse. This perspective on the importance of this choice is supported by all sorts of data ranging from surveys of the predictors of life satisfaction, to studies of the course of psychiatric syndromes, to the quest for personal meaning. Who one chooses to spend their life with and the nature of the co-constructed relationship is, arguably, the most important adult experience most of us encounter. It makes our relative lack of a comprehensive understanding of the crucial elements of such decision-making all the more remarkable.

These thoughts—many of them presented in earlier columns—returned to me in my rereading books that have touched me deeply earlier in my life. Here I will describe one; the haunting story of a bad marital choice (really two of such) presented in Wendell Berry's wonderful novel, *The Memory of Old Jack* (2). In our relative ignorance of the multiple factors that account for such tragic choices, we can continue to learn from the works of great novelists.

Old Jack is in his 80s and failing. The novel is about his recollections of his life, those experiences that shaped who he came to be. Born in 1860 he devoted his adult years to working the family farm. Jack is now living in a hotel with other old persons in Berry's fictional small town of Port William, Kentucky. It is Jack's intense attraction and marriage to Ruth and their shared inability to resolve their differences that indelibly scars his life. Jack, when in his late 20s, has reworked his family's failed farm and finds fundamental pleasure in working the land and filled with pride in his success. He is also a lady's man, strongly influenced by physical passion. He is drawn to Ruth's beauty, perhaps particularly his sense that he can arouse her from her reticence. Ruth, in turn, came from a family that had left the land and turned to the pursuits of town. Jack's devotion to his land was not seen positively by Ruth, nor was she comfortable with her own or his sexuality. Wendell Berry describes this mismatch in wonderful prose, and I will quote him liberally.

"He won her with his vices. She accepted him as a sort of 'mission field', and it was the great disaster of both their lives. He bound her to him by disavowing the very energy that bound him to her. She was bound to him by a vision of him that she held above him—that he, in fact, neither understood nor aspired to; and he was bound to her by a vision of her that she would discover, by her own rights, to be beneath her. Her ambition would be forever as strange and estranging to him as the great heat and strength of his desire would be to her" (2, p. 51).

Berry speaks to the tragic impasse created by two strong persons who cannot agree on the terms of their relationship. "They were extraordinary people, those two. Had it not been so, had they not been so evenly matched, their contest—for that is what it was—might have ended short of marriage. As it was, it had to go on, it had to accept the terms of a final defeat for them both" (2, p. 51, 52).

Berry describes the consequences of such poor choices, of not really knowing who the other is. If the partners are both of strong will the result is either chronic conflict or emotional disengagement. Either outcome is a tragedy. What are its products? Here we only know of those for Jack. He not only fails to have a partner who validates that which is central to his sense of self, but he, too, comes to doubt their importance. "He no longer seemed to himself to be enough. He knew that he had been found wanting in Ruth's eyes, which meant, since her eyes had become the only qualification of his, that he was now found wanting in his own. Her judgment of him, however he might have resented and defied it, had entered into him, and the judgment was that though he might have pride and desire . . . he had, properly speaking, no ambition" (2, p. 65).

And so Jack was changed in a fundamental way: he no longer so valued what his life had been built upon. He took Ruth's perceptions of him into his self. Despite their ongoing conflict—usually surfacing about the more trivial aspects of a shared life—he incorporated her view of him as deficient. How common this outcome may be in relationships of otherwise admirable individuals is hard to know. Two relatively well-functioning adults can construct a relationship damaging to both, and the possibility of adult growth may be impeded.

Psychotherapists of my generation—almost all of whom were psychoanalytic to one degree or another—characteristically looked to childhood experiences to help explain adult outcomes. Relationships during adult life could be understood as emanating from early developmental experiences within the childhood family. There was a strong propensity to repeat, and, unless healing relationships occurred after childhood, the therapist could understand the patient's current relationship dilemma as his or her unconscious re-creation of or defense from the distant past. Although such linear thinking has declined, it is, perhaps, no surprise that in my rereading of old Jack, my thoughts about why Jack made such a tragic choice and stayed with it focused on his childhood. And, of course, Berry provides what I was looking for. Jack's two older brothers were killed in the Civil War, his mother died in some sort of grief-induced illness, and his father retreated into silence. All of this before Jack was six! A child experiencing such horrific losses will not readily enter into intimate adult relationships —the underlying fear is too great. He or she thus selects safety over closeness, predictability over encounter. Jack's outcome is sealed by age six.

The explanation is too pat. It may have some validity but it almost certainly is far from the whole story. It doesn't explain, for example Jack's midlife love affair with a young widow whom he clearly believed valued him for who he was not who she wanted or needed him to be. We do not know the extent of Jack's expressed vulnerability with this more loving woman, but Berry tells us that this relationship became a central priority for Jack, and his grief profound when she died in a house fire.

The truth of the matter is that we do not understand bad choices, at least in any comprehensive way. Our understanding of their impact on life satisfaction and life meaning exceeds our knowledge of how they come to be. Psychotherapists, however, seek explanations—it is, perhaps, a distinguishing characteristic of our vocation. My reading of Berry's novel is that old Jack would not have been a good subject for psychotherapeutic explorations of his life. On his own he came to the conclusion, however, that he bore his share of responsibility for the tragic marital outcome. In doing so, Berry suggests, he became more whole. Whether this is the author's redemptive narrative strategy—making something good out of something bad—is up to the reader to decide.

References

1. Lewis, J.M. (2002). "The Roads Less Traveled." Psychiatric Times, Practicing Column, September. Reprinted in *Reflections: On Relationships With Self and Others,* 2009.
2. Berry, W. (1974). *The Memory of Old Jack.* San Diego: Harcourt Bruce Jovanovich.

October 2008

27

HELPING EACH OTHER ALONG

"Do you never get fed up with his behavior?" I asked the wife. "No," she responded, "It is not his fault. He tries hard to be a good person, but is easily tempted." "And you?" I said to him, "Does the grief you bring to her ever bother you?" "Of course," he responded and with a broad smile added, "She's a saint —always there for me."

Robert Penn Warren wrote, "There is nothing women love so much as the drunkard, the hellion, the roarer, the reprobate. They love him because they —women, I mean —are like bees in Samson's parable in the Bible: They like to build their honeycomb in the carcass of a dead lion" (1, p. 365). Although Warren may have caught a piece of the dynamics, the tradeoffs in such relationships are usually much more complex.

Psychotherapists who see couples occasionally observe those whose relationships qualify for the "Saint and Sinner" designation. At a recent academic grand rounds such a couple was presented to me, and, although the resident presenting the clinical information focused on the question of the husband's diagnosis ("was he bipolar or a sociopath?"), the material lent itself better to a discussion of saints and sinners.

During the past 10 years, I have seen a half dozen such situations, and because understanding this relationship pattern forces one to examine a number of important theoretical issues at the interface of individual and relationship functioning, it seems a useful topic for this column.

First, though, a brief summary of the clinical characteristics of the saints and sinners relationship pattern. More often than not the sinner is the man and the saint his female partner. Regardless of gender, however, the sinner usually reports a childhood filled with rejection, neglect, or abuse and the early development of an oppositional pattern of behavior. He or she often becomes the "bad" child in the family. Early delinquent behavior appears to be the anlage of adult petty crime, vocational instability, drug abuse, and multiple infidelities. Usually the narcissistic aspects of personality structure—"the usual rules do not apply to me"—are easy to observe.

The saintly partner most often describes a childhood in which one or both parents were absent or chronically disabled, and she or he assumed a parentified, caretaking role. The saint-to-be can be understood as having sacrificed much of childhood in the service of attaining the identity of the "good" child.

In their adult interactions saints and sinners demonstrate a characteristic pattern. Each partner avoids the ambivalence inherent in adult relationships. The sinner denies the harmful impact of his or her behavior on the saint, and the saint, in turn, denies enabling such behavior by refusing to set clear limits on the sinner. The sinner may acknowledge the felt safety he or she experiences in the relationship all the while denying that his or her behavior repetitiously tests that safety. The saint most often expresses the idea that the sinner is not malevolent, but sick or, in some way, the victim of forces beyond control. Some saints express the belief that their role is divinely inspired, a mission given to them by God. This felt specialness may be the surface manifestation of an underlying grandiosity which, in turn, is linked to deeply repressed doubts about personal worth. Regardless of the underlying dynamics, the relationship pattern is often remarkably stable and resistant to therapeutic interventions.

The stability or relatively fixed nature of the pattern can best be understood as a reflection of the importance of the individual needs that the pattern serves. No individual need is understood as more important from the viewpoint of the psychology of the self than the maintenance of a coherent sense of self. There is growing appreciation that maintaining a coherent sense of self relies in part on receiving messages from important others that verify that sense of self. An important body of recent research suggests that individuals are drawn to others who re-enforce their senses of self, even if such is negative! (2-4). Those with a basically negative sense of self are understood as caught between the need for self-enhancement and the need for self-verification. And, more often than not, the latter need wins. From the perspective of self-verification theory the saint and sinner each find acceptance of their respective good and bad identities. The relationship serves the purpose of helping each partner maintain a coherent sense of self.

Another relationship process illustrated by the saint and sinner pattern involves projection and projective identification. Some of us who study and treat couples believe that these processes operate in all important relationships and can be considered pathological only to the extent that they bind one or both partners to fixed and maladaptive roles. Saints can thus be understood as projecting their deeply repressed anger to their sinner partners and behaving in ways that facilitate its expression in that partner's behavior. Sinners are understood as projecting their underlying wish to feel good or competent to their saintly partners and then evoking such behaviors in the partner. From the perspective of projection and projective identification, saints and sinners are understood as caught up in a massive and mutual process that maintains their respective, if severely limited, identities.

Another perspective on this relationship pattern involves its role in impeding or preventing adult psychological maturation. Much of current thinking about adult development involves the use of multiple markers of maturity. The capacity to use mature defenses in resolving conflict, the ability to regulate affects, and the achievement of intimate relationships are examples. A marker of particular interest is the ability to sustain internal contradictions. Here the reference is to the inevitable human polarities. We hurt those we love; we believe we are safely in charge of our lives and yet must face our helplessness in certain situations; we are capable of acts of genuine altruism but also of extreme self-centeredness; we move inexorably to aging and death and yet long for youth and immortality. The list is longer, but these four are illustrative. The mature person is understood as recognizing and tolerating these contradictions rather than resolving them through acceptance of only one side of each polarity.

In this struggle to sustain these inevitable internal contradictions, a sensitive, responsive partner may play an important role. Through caring and gentle confrontations he or she can assist in the recognition and acceptance of these human polarities. To feel loved by a partner who recognizes these contradictions is a major step in the acceptance of an expanded and more complex sense of one's self.

This marker of adult maturity cannot be readily reached if one has constructed a central relationship in which the contradictions are mutually avoided. The saint and sinner pattern is a striking example of how a jointly constructed relationship may impede successful adult development.

How can these comments about saints and sinners be helpful to clinicians? More than any other way they inform as to the importance of a patient's central relationship in influencing both the course of psychiatric syndromes and the response to treatment interventions. Understanding that saints and sinners help each other along by verifying and maintaining each partner's coherent sense of self often means that the pattern itself must be altered before individual change can occur. Treating the couple and their relationship pattern directly is more apt to be helpful than treating each partner and his and her symptoms individually. Indeed, an individual approach may miss the importance of the relationship pattern.

References

1. Warren, RP. (1996). *All The King's Men*. Harvest Books: Harcourt Brace and Co., Orlando, Fl, 2nd Edition, (originally published 1946).
2. Swann, W.B., Hixon, J.G., De LaRoude, C. (1992). "Embracing The BitterTruth": Negative Self-Concepts and Marital Commitment. Psychological. *Science*, 3:2, 118-121, March, 1992.
3. Swann, W.B., De La Roude C., Hixon J.G. (1994). "Authenticity and Positivity Strivings in Marriage and Courtship." Journal of Personality and Social Psychology, 66:5, 392-401.
4. Pelham, B.W., Swann, W.B. (1994). "The Juncture of Intrapersonal and Interpersonal Knowledge: Self-Certainty and Interpersonal Congruence." Personality and Social Psychology Bulletin, 20:4, 349-357, August.

May 2002

28

WHAT KEEPS THEM TOGETHER?

> They had been married for 30 years, and I was the first therapist they had seen for what was jointly described as 30 years of hell. Their chronic conflict took many forms but could be best described as shared nastiness. Each blamed the other for the relationship failure using the language of undesirable personality traits.
>
> At the same time, both were successful professionals and described long-term, conflict-free relationships with siblings, friends and colleagues. Neither demonstrated symptoms suggesting significant individual psychopathology. They seemed to be individuals of average mental health who had jointly constructed a painful relationship that neither had shown any inclination to leave.

If you ask such couples, in light of their shared misery, what has kept them together, many respond by saying they do not know. Others indicate that concern for their children or economic factors have played a role. A few cite religious factors; "Jesus has placed me in this marriage for a reason, and I have yet to discover just what it is," is an example given by a successful attorney.

Although some persons in chronically conflicted marriages enter into often sustained sexual affairs with others, a surprising number do not. Many of the partners, however, describe psychologically intimate relationships with others. "I can talk with my brother, Jim, about anything—we have a very close relationship," an internist in a chronically conflicted marriage reflected as we explored his capacity for psychological intimacy.

Although it is important to respect and explore each partner's statements about remaining in the unhappy marriage, clinicians also need to have a theoretical perspective which can help explore the unconscious individual and relationship dynamics that may underlie both the conflict and the durability of each relationship. It is to that end that this column is directed.

A starting point is the promise that each adult can be understood as having needs for both separateness and connectedness (1). The strength of these needs varies from individual to individual and is often noted most dramatically under circumstances of a perceived threat as in the approach-avoidance paradigm. An adult's balance of the need for separateness and connectedness is determined by many factors. There is almost certainly a genetic component, and autism may well represent an extreme example of a biologic propensity for separateness. Early attachment experiences also play a role. Recall that most studies of infant-mother attachment demonstrate that about 20 percent of infants are seen as avoidant and this attachment pattern has been shown to persist into adolescence for many. The family one is reared in may also have considerable impact on the developing capacities for separateness and connectedness. Some families encourage separateness (autonomy and competition); others emphasize connectedness (empathy and intimacy); and others encourage both separateness and connectedness depending on the context. Some children internalize these family norms and others struggle against them. Different cultural groups may also place greater emphasis on one of the needs (agency or community).

In clinical practice patients with unusually strong propensities for either separateness or connectedness (loners or those with excessive "dependent" behaviors) often report painful childhood experiences in which either retreating from or moving towards important others had adaptive value.

When two persons enter a relationship with a hoped-for lasting nature, the issue of what each brings in the way of needs for separateness and connectedness can be crucial in determining how the relationship goes. There is apt to be a smooth course if the partners' needs are similar. Once the endorphin phase of the relationship wanes, however, differences may become apparent. Often one partner—more often but not always the woman—wants more closeness than the other partner. Each partner may try to impose his or her definition of the balance of separateness and connectedness on the other. Some partners succeed, and the resulting power imbalance results in what may be called a dominant—submissive relationship. Often the "defeated" partner accepts her or his fate because of the ways in which the relationship meets other needs. "He is a stable, caring, person who provides well" and "she is a funny and charming partner who is an excellent mother" are examples.

Some couples over time negotiate a compromise that involves partial fulfillment of each partner's need for separateness and connectedness. "It's a lot better than it used to be," one woman reported, "he has learned to listen to me, and I have come to better accept that he is just unable to be deeply in touch with himself."

If one has the opportunity to study couples who do not come for help, examples of "healing" relationships are common, "I was such a loner and she (he) has taught me how to be close" and "I would never have become my own person without his (her) encouragement" are examples. There are longitudinal studies that document the healing impact of some relationships (2).

Our central concern here, however, is chronically conflicted relationships and their durability. How can the persistence of such relationships be understood? First, clinical work with such couples reveals that most often both partners fear psychological intimacy and have learned in childhood that avoidance of the vulnerability that inevitably comes with deep self-disclosure protects from harm. Although one partner may yearn more openly for a strong, connection, he or she may feel safe in the knowledge of the other partner's unavailability.

A second clinical premise is that one unconscious purpose of conflict is to produce distance in the relationship. Often it appears that conflict is provoked after an experience of some closeness. It is as if the moments or period of greater closeness leads to fear, then anger. The anger re-establishes the more comfortable psychological distance. Chronically conflicted relationships can thus be understood as providing the partners with a modicum of connectedness all the while avoiding the vulnerability of closeness. One is not quite alone and trades off happiness for the safety that anger-provoked distance may bring.

Some of these relationships are remarkably resistant to clinical interventions. The interlocking projections seem indelibly fixed. Others, however, respond to the therapist's efforts to stop the blaming and to begin to experiment with vulnerable self-disclosure in the safety of the therapeutic situation. Often but modest increases in closeness make for increased satisfaction. "Although we really don't talk about deeper feelings, we enjoy each other more and have far fewer arguments—so things are clearly better," one husband reported at the termination of couples therapy. Other couples with comparable gains want to continue sessions at reduced frequency. "These sessions are a safety zone for us. We can replay those times when our differences lead to painful conflicts. We don't want to stop them completely," another spouse reported.

The decision to offer treatment to couples with chronically conflicted relationships can be justified by the known effects of such relationships on the partners. It is difficult to meet the challenges of individual adult development in the context of a chronically conflicted marriage, and symptoms (e.g. depression, alcohol abuse) may develop that can come to play a role in the struggle to have more of one's way in the definition of the relationship.

Some survey data reveal that many persons' life satisfaction and sense of personal meaning are derived from marital and family relationships. Chronically conflicted relationships remove this source of satisfaction and meaning.

Further, there is evidence suggesting that a chronically conflicted parental relationship can impede the healthy development of children exposed to such unhappy circumstances.

Marriage or other lasting relationships offer the individuals the chance to redo painful experiences from early life, to restart blocked developmental trajectories, to better regulate impulses, affects and cognitions, to enhance cellular immune mechanisms, and to better search for life satisfaction and meaning. When such relationships succeed they often transform. When they fail they often cast a poll on all of life. Those who are spending their adult lives in conflict with their partners over the definition of the relationship are missing that which is possible in human relationships. They deserve our attention, our understanding, and the best of our therapeutic efforts.

References

1. Lewis, J.M. (1997). *Marriage as a Search for Healing: Theory, Assessment, and Therapy*. New York: Brunner-Mazel.
2. Rutter, M. Quinton D. (1984). "Long-term follow-up of women institutionalized in childhood: factors promoting good functioning in adult life." Br J of Devel Psych, 18:225-234.

January 2003

29

CIRCLE OF DISCONNECTION

He called and said the problem was his wife's anger. "She has the shortest fuse in the world; her anger erupts all the time, and I am her favorite target. It goes back to her parents and their self-centered neglect of her." I suggested to him that they come together for an exploratory couples interview. He said that he would try but that several previous efforts had failed after a single session when she had refused to return for another appointment.

They came, and, in their fifties, both were attractive, bright, and clearly successful. He defined the central problem as her anger. She responded with open anger but quickly pointed out how unavailable he was. "He pays no attention to me. He is totally involved in his legal practice and playing golf. When home he is constantly on the computer. If I try to talk with him, he continues to look at the screen. Furthermore, he hasn't touched me in many years—no hugs, kisses, let alone making love. I'm totally alone, and, of course, I'm furious much of the time."

This interactional pattern of unavailability—anger and/or depression is a common one in the couples I see. The details may differ but one partner is truly unavailable and the other either chronically angry or depressed. It is useful to think of unavailability as actual (not being physically present), attentional (present physically but always involved in individual pursuits), and emotional (showing no interest in the partner's subjective reality). Often all or some combination of the three are present. The other partner's anger or depression (or some combination of both) is also clear. If his or her psychological status is more open anger than depression, it is often easier to work with, perhaps because it can be understood as something other than a more passive giving-up.

Despite the differing details couples caught up in this pattern show some similarities. These include a sole or major focus on the other's contribution to the pattern and an avoidance or minimization of one's own participation. Further, the focus on the other's characteristics are, for the most part, accurate. The unavailable partner is really unavailable; the angry partner's anger is equally real.

A second similarity is that, there are almost always reported childhood experiences that can be understood as leading to adult attachment patterns of either unavailability or anger. As such the current unavailable—anger or depressed interactional pattern can be considered as an unfortunate repetition of painful childhood experiences.

A third similarity is that the interactional pattern has often intensified after one or both partners have lost an important relationship. The last child leaving home, the death of a close friend, or a favorite sibling moving away are examples. The pattern becomes worse at a time when most couples have to depend more on their relationship for support and closeness.

Treatment of couples with the unavailability—anger pattern is based on several principles. The first principle is to emphasize the circularity of their interactions. One partner is unavailable and this leads to the other partner's anger which in turn leads to greater unavailability, more anger, and the circular dynamics become entrenched. As a consequence the partners share responsibility for their dilemma. I make it clear that, although their observations about each other seem mostly valid, a continuing focus on each other's undesirable characteristics (blaming) is nonproductive and continues the circular pattern.

In all of this I try to introduce them to an interactional rather than a personality-based way of looking at their dilemma. Doing so, I inform them, is empowering. As long as you see the problem as reflecting your partner's personality, you are helpless. If, however, you see his or her unavailability or anger as responsive to your behavior you are not helpless.

In my approach to such couples I ask them for guidelines for change. "How would you like him (or her) to be more available?" and "When would you most like her (or him) to not respond angrily?" I usually incorporate these wishes into a behavioral prescription. Twenty minutes a day of undivided attention to each other's experience of the day, a hug when separating and reuniting each day, dinner out once a week, and, often later, the gradual reintroduction of some forms of physical touching and holding are some of the ingredients of the prescription. Another part of this type of intervention is to encourage the angry partner to use the language of vulnerability. "It hurts when you don't pay attention to me" is less apt to increase one's partner's unavailability than is an angry outburst.

Most of these couples have never learned to listen closely to each other, to help the other explore whatever he or she needs to talk about. I give them written instructions on exploratory conversations and ask them to tape such conversations at home and bring them to the office. We listen to these initial tapes and they are usually painful examples of not being there for an important other. They are filled with inattention, advice-giving, and judgmental responses. Hearing oneself converse in this way is often a painful experience, and both partners need support and encouragement to learn a new and different conversational format.

Another intervention in this approach is going over and trying to rescript between sessions episodes of the familiar circle of unavailability and anger. "What might you have said at this point that would have signaled greater availability?" and "How could you have used the language of vulnerability rather than exploding as you did?" may lead to useful rescripting.

These interventions are helpful to many couples with this interactional pattern. It is often better to focus initially on increasing the availability (actual, attentional, and emotional) of the unavailable partner because he or she can be given concrete suggestions about becoming more available. "See if she (he) is less angry if you listen to her 20 minutes each evening" is a suggestion that can take the form of specific behavioral prescriptions. If helpful the interventions result in a stronger interactional focus with less blaming the partner for his or her negative personality traits.

Collaborative problem-solving can be emphasized and conflict about differences of opinion reduced. Some of these couples begin to experiment with more psychological intimacy than ever before. Partners can become more available to each other and soften or relinquish characteristic ways of relating.

These changing patterns of relating are sometimes associated with evidence of individual maturation. Learning more about one's participation in relationship patterns is learning about one's relational self. This learning can facilitate change across a broad variety of psychological characteristics including better affect regulation and increased cognitive complexity. It is, perhaps, something like this that Toni Morrison described in her novel, Beloved (1). When Sixto was asked why he walked 30 miles each way to see his girlfriend on weekends, he said that she was a "friend of his mind"—that is, she helped him sort out better what he thought and felt. I like to think that one of the ways a couples approach helps to disrupt the circle of disconnectedness is that it encourages each partner to become for the other a better friend of the mind.

Reference

1. Morrison, T. (1988). *Beloved.* New York: Plume Printing.

March 2006

30

TOO CLOSE?

She is a psychiatric social worker, and we have known each other for years through having served together on several community boards. Her call was about her sister, the wife of a small town physician. The story she told involved her brother-in-law's massive coronary and continuing hospitalization in intensive care. Her sister had developed what sounded like an acute psychosis—disorganized speech, inability to care for herself, and severe agitation.

My social worker-friend described her sister's marriage as intense and exclusive. "She works in his office so they're always together. When you're with them there is a kind of wall around them. They seem glued together. It's been that way since the very beginning of their relationship. Almost immediately they began using "we" and "us" all the time—no "I" or "Me." They never wanted children, said they had all they needed with each other."

She brought her sister to see me, and it was quickly apparent that the sister was acutely psychotic. During her three weeks of hospitalization she improved somewhat with medication, and, as she did, shared with me the delusion that the man in intensive care was not her husband but an imposter.

Her physician—husband survived and three weeks later stormed into my office angrily demanding his wife's release "There's not a damn thing wrong with her," he told me, and despite my efforts to empathize with his anxiety about their separation and to emphasize her need for continuing care, he removed her from the hospital.

A year later I ran into my social worker-friend and asked about her sister. "Who knows?" she responded. "If anything they're even more isolated than before. They won't talk to me because I brought her to see you."

This overly brief clinical vignette illustrates the hazards of enmeshed relationships, particularly the participants' inability to tolerate separation without adverse consequences. Before turning to a description of the dynamics of enmeshed relationships, however, the question of whether such relationships are abnormal needs to be addressed. The answer is that it depends on how normal marriages are defined. If longevity is used as a marker of normality, enmeshed relationships qualify in that they are most often long-lasting.

Marital satisfaction is a widely used marker of the quality of a marriage. Each spouse separately completes a questionnaire, and, if both spouses have high scores, the marriage is considered successful. Partners in enmeshed marriages almost invariably score their relationships as highly satisfactory.

It is only when a more telling yardstick is used that enmeshed marriages are understood as dysfunctional. The yardstick is the concept that a marriage "should" provide the psychological milieu that encourages the continuing maturation of both partners and facilitates the healthy development of children raised by the couple. This yardstick, admittedly a value judgment, is the one used in our research at the Timberlawn Research Foundation and by other, although not all, marital—family research teams.

Enmeshed marriages do not provide the context for individual maturation. They appear to be relationships in which both partners sacrifice their sense of a clear, separate, and autonomous identity to become a fused "we." The clinical presumption is that the partners were drawn to each other by pre-existing severe ego deficits, although disentangling antecedents and consequences through longitudinal studies has not, to my knowledge, been accomplished. In part this is because such couples avoid emotional involvement with others and, as a consequence, rarely, if ever, present for couples therapy or volunteer for marital-family research. The few such relationships I have seen involved, as in the couple described, when separation threatened the fusion or, when, an adolescent child of enmeshed parents was referred—usually mandated by the school system—often because of bizarre behavior.

Enmeshed relationships illustrate (in the negative) one pathway through which individual growth may occur as a consequence of adult relationships. The reference here is to the negotiation of differences. Enmeshed couples struggle to deny differences in affects and thoughts in the attempt to construct a sameness—a "we-ness" that obliterates individual differences, often protecting against a presumed dangerous world. Relationships that facilitate individual growth acknowledge differences, even come to cherish them, and in dealing with them acknowledge the individuality of both partners. Thus, respect for each other's subjective reality can lead to affirmation of each partner's authentic self. Additionally, respecting the ways in which one's partner is different may lead to getting more deeply in touch with similar but denied aspects of one's self.

The dynamics of enmeshed relationships has largely been attributed to shared individual ego deficits. Other theoretical perspectives, however, suggest different interpretations. The attachment perspective suggests that an enmeshed outcome might result from the coming together of two persons with anxious adult attachment patterns who cling to each other tightly to avoid feared rejection. An existential perspective might focus on unusually intense and shared anxiety about the ultimate concern of existential isolation. Separateness, from this perspective, is tantamount to death. Although other theoretical explanations are equally relevant and may be useful, the truth is that we do not know what predispositions may operate in the formation of enmeshed relationships.

Many such enmeshed couples decide not to have children, and those who do appear to either incorporate the child into their enmeshed system or exclude the child, making the child an outsider in his or her own family. The child's development is apt to be significantly impeded in either situation. In the former, the development of a clear identity as a separate and autonomous being is impaired. This circumstance—the enmeshed family—was found during the early days of family research to be one family type in families containing children with schizophrenic spectrum disorders.

The psychological fate of the excluded child is not clearly known.

Some adult psychotherapy patients describe such parental relationships, and, unless another and secure attachment figure was present during childhood, are apt to struggle with profound disturbances in their sense of self and capacity for relating to others. The distinguished researcher of the borderline syndromes, John Gunderson, told me years ago that a common family structure of the borderline patients he studied was an enmeshed parental relationship with the patient-to-be excluded from the enmeshed system.

Thus, it is when enmeshed marriages are viewed from the perspective of facilitating the continued adult maturation of both partners and providing the psychological context conducive to the healthy development of any children they raise that their dysfunctionality stands out.

Although how one views enmeshed marriages is dependent upon the perspective used (longevity, satisfaction, or individual maturation), such relationships serve to remind us that the marital relationship is the major opportunity most of us have to continue to grow as adults. Such growth involves both the capacity to relate closely and the ability to function autonomously. Enmeshed marriages discourage autonomy by keeping each partner's identity completely embedded in the relationship. It is possible to be too close.

May 2004

Part III

On Psychotherapy

31

TO HEAR THE CRY OF BATS

Julia:
". . . And he had a remarkable sense of hearing.
The only man I ever met who could hear the cry of bats." (1, p. 13)

His mother had died when he was six; his wife left him and their daughter for another man ten years ago, and two months before our appointment he had taken his daughter to a distant city to begin her college years. In the time since separating from his daughter he had felt a sad emptiness, had trouble sleeping, and his diminished appetite had resulted in a ten pound weight loss. His internist prescribed an antidepressant without, however, any relief—hence the referral to me.

The major theme of being left by women stood out so clearly and seemed so obvious that it was natural to wonder what is ramifications were. The following interchange occurred in our second session:

Patient: ". . .and, so, it was the right thing for Pam (his daughter) to do—the scholarship is such an honor—and the school is much superior to the local colleges."
Therapist: "It all makes such good sense—a very logical decision." (a beginning approach to his denial).
Patient: "Yeah." (without obvious feeling)
Therapist: (after a long silence) "And, yet, it's since she left that things have gone downhill—"(a more direct approach to his denial)

Patient: "Yeah." (again, flatly, followed by more silence)

The immediate decision is whether to honor or further confront his denial of feelings about the loss of his daughter. His brief responses and long silences after my initial attempts suggested his strong need to sustain the denial. Would it be safer to explore the earlier losses of mother and wife? Could he deal more openly with past affects or are they inseparable from those concerning the here-and-now loss of his daughter?

Therapist: (interrupting a long silence) "Well, you've really had tough luck with women leaving you—" ("tough luck" chosen deliberately to avoid any hint of what I suspected might be underlying self-blame)

Patient: "I don't think it was so much tough luck with my wife. I was pretty unavailable—not very attentive, and she tried hard to let me know—that is before she got involved with him."

Therapist: "Sounds like you sort of blame yourself for that loss."

Patient: "Yeah—but it's not unusual for me to blame myself—it's kind of part of my personality. I'm really hard on myself."

Here was a beginning to a series of useful explorations centering about avoidance of anger, his intrapunitiveness, and resulting self-blame for his losses. Over the course of months he worked with increasing affect regarding his wife's abandoning both him and his daughter. We never were able to recapture his presumed self-blame about his mother's death. At length, however, he did explore his anger at his daughter for choosing the scholarship at a prestigious college and leaving him. His symptoms gradually cleared, and he decided to stop regular sessions, to call if he felt the need.

There is much that could be said about this not unusual piece of psychotherapeutic work. What I wish to focus on here, however, is the therapist's need to hear the cry of bats.

I recalled Eliot's metaphor while exploring the literature on the psychotherapist as wounded healer. The underlying theme of unique sensitivity growing out of personal anguish was present throughout the literature, although with little, if any, empirical foundation. I found that the most often cited sources were replete with all sorts of definitional, sampling, and measurement errors. In short, there was scant empirical evidence that the psychotherapist's sensitivity was (or had to be) based on his or her own problems. To hear the cry of bats, however, seemed to capture both sides of the cultural ambivalence about therapists: their abilities to hear what others cannot (sensitivity) and to hear what isn't there (craziness).

If, then, to hear the cry of bats—as in hearing the not so obvious—does not necessarily arise from the anguish of the wounded healer, where does it come from? Years ago as a teacher of psychotherapeutic process I devised a series of experiential exercises that asked beginning residents to place themselves temporarily in the experience of others as portrayed in both audiotape and videotaped material (2). It was quickly apparent that some residents could do this better than others: they had come into training with greater empathic skills. We do not know how such skills evolve, but it is likely that a concert of factors are at play, including genetically determined brain systems, early experiences of attunement with a sensitive mother, and growing up in a family that encouraged affective expression and responsiveness. Regardless of its complex origins, the ability to relax momentarily one's own ego boundaries and take in the experience of another and, then, let the other know something of what one has experienced must be an important dimension of hearing the cry of bats. Although this ability exists to one extent or another in all persons, it is only in psychotherapists (and a few other occupations) that it is an essential distinction.

Another root of the ability to hear the cry of bats is a seasoned knowledge of psychodynamics. In the brief snips of my work with the man noted above I was clearly relying on an awareness that the dynamics of some depressive disorders involve the turning onto the self of anger at the lost other. This formulation—going back to the earlier days of psychoanalysis—is, however, like all other generic formulations a two-edged sword in that they can be indiscriminately applied to those for whom there is no fit. Perhaps the wisest position is to consider such formulations as tentative clinical hypotheses that need careful testing in the psychotherapeutic interchange.

A third source of the ability to hear the cry of bats is a more radical idea: Hearing the cry of bats is better considered a characteristic of certain relationships than it is an individual characteristic. From this perspective it takes two to tango. There can be moments in the interaction between two (or more) persons when there is a remarkable coming together, an intense and shared emotional experience, an existential encounter, or an I:Thou duet. The participation of both partners is required, and the empathic moment is best considered an emergent property of the relationship; that is, not completely predictable on the basis of either partner's individual characteristics.

Regardless of the fact that we may not understand completely the multiple roots of this ability, it seems wise in the current climate of descriptive diagnose and directive interviewing to recall that not very long ago to hear the cry of bats was considered an important characteristic of the psychiatrist.

References

1. Eliot, T.S. (1950). *The Cocktail Party.* New York: Harcourt, Brace & World, Inc.
2. Lewis, J.M. (1991). *Swimming Upstream: Teaching and Learning Psychotherapy in a Biological Era.* New York: Brunner-Mazel.

March 2005

32

FIRST CITIZENS OF CONTINGENCY

She was seen at the request of her psychologist—friend six months after the death of her husband who was killed by a drunk driver. Her grief was unrelenting: she rarely got out of bed until late in the day, and her weight loss was marked. She appeared immobilized by sadness and described waves of alternating emptiness and rage. Her symptoms had not responded to several antidepressants prescribed by her internist. There had been other losses in the past 18 months. She had been laid off from her job as an associate corporate attorney when the corporation had decided to do away with an in-house legal department. Before that yet another attempt at invitro fertilization had failed. Although shaken by these experiences, it sounded as if she had functioned well prior to her husband's death.

There was no history of depressive disorders in her family, nor early losses that might have sensitized her in some way to later losses. Her life appeared to be relatively uneventful—save for the inability to get pregnant—and she described her marriage as very compatible. Her relationships with family and friends suggested a supportive interpersonal environment, and there was nothing to indicate chronic problems with self-esteem. In short, there were none of the obvious markers of unusual vulnerability to depressive disorders.

Why, then, had her grief merged into a major depression? One perspective is that, in light of her succession of losses, anyone could become depressed; there is, therefore, no indication for further searching. Try other antidepressants, combine them with anticonvulsants, the right combination will bring her relief. For the psychotherapist (or, at least, some of them), however, this perspective is not adequate. He or she is drawn to contingency and wishes to explore and understand the connections between the patient's depression and her inner life, relationship world, and losses. Contingency, in the sense used here, involves the understanding of close, causal connections.

It is surely this definition that Robert Pinsky wrote about in his poem, Essay on Psychiatrists, describing psychiatrists as the "first citizens of contingency" (1, p. 58). In this quest to understand connections we are, Pinsky tells us, "Far from the doctrinaire past of the old ones" (1, p. 58). I recalled Pinsky's poem and thought about the importance of contingency again when I read several recent studies of genetic-environment interactions in psychopathology. These studies demonstrate that the expression of genes is influenced by environmental processes and that genetic influences on psychopathology may be indirect in the sense of influencing the person's responses to stress (2, 3).

These studies by Caspi and his colleagues are from the Dunedin Longitudinal Study in New Zealand of 1037 persons who were studied on multiple occasions from age 3 to age 26. The first study investigated the relationships between antisocial behavior, maltreatment during childhood, and genetic activity. The gene involved was Monoamine Oxidase A (MAOA), which encodes the MAOA enzyme, which metabolizes important neurotransmitters rendering them inactive. Individual differences at a functional polymorphism in the promoter of the MAOA gene were used to identify genetic susceptibility. The hypothesis was that the MAOA genotype can moderate the effects of childhood maltreatment on the neural systems involved in antisocial behavior.

The study clearly demonstrates that in maltreated children low MAOA activity clearly increases the subsequent development of conduct disorder, antisocial behaviors, disposition toward violence, and conviction for violent offenses. Low MAOA activity without maltreatment did not predict these outcomes, but 85 percent of low MAOA activity subjects whose maltreatment was severe developed antisocial behavior. Further, high MAOA activity protected against the development of antisocial behaviors in maltreated subjects. It is important to note that the maltreated children (36% of the sample) and those who were not maltreated did not differ on MAOA activity: thus, the maltreatment was not a parental response to the children's MAOA genotype.

This remarkable study of contingencies brings to light new connections between experiences, specific genetic activity, and psychopathology. It also raises fascinating questions, one of which is how and in what form the experience of childhood maltreatment is stored in the brain so that, in its interaction with low MAOA activity, its effects become obvious years later. Is the experience stored as a frightening cognitive complex, an inner working model of an insecure or disorganized attachment, or are its effects moderated through the maltreatment's impact on important developmental processes such as affect regulation or moral development?

Caspi and his colleagues made a step in the direction of clarifying the processes that shape how genetic activity influences psychopathology in their study of the development of depression in the Dunedin sample (3). In this investigation they studied depression, stressful life events, and the serotonin transporter (5—HTT) gene. This gene is involved in the reuptake of serotonin in brain synapses. The promoter activity of this gene is modified depending on the presence of short and long alleles. Their subjects either had two short alleles, one short and one long alleles, or two long alleles. Stressful life events between the 21st and 26th birthdays were systematically recorded. Depression was ascertained using a standard interview schedule and informant reports.

Their hypothesis was that stressful life events would lead to depression more frequently in those subjects who had either one or two short alleles of the 5—HTT gene. Their hypothesis was confirmed in that of those experiencing the most stressful life experiences 33 percent with a short 5—HTT allele developed depression compared to 17 percent of those with two long alleles. The same relationship held for the probability of suicidal ideology and attempts. It is important to note that the presence of a short allele of 5—HTT gene did not predict depression in the absence of life stress.

The study also demonstrates that childhood maltreatment led to early adult depression only in those subjects carrying a short allele of the 5–HTT gene. In contrast and as noted, childhood maltreatment in those subjects with a low activity MAOA gene were at risk for the development of antisocial behaviors. Although it is far too soon for any firm conclusions, it may turn out that the same adverse experiences can result in different clinical syndromes depending on the individual's genotype.

It is hard to ask for more from such exciting investigations, but wouldn't it be wonderful to see included in such designs measurements of both intrapsychic and interpersonal variables demonstrated to influence the development of psychopathology? Attachment style, level of ego maturity, and the presence of supportive relationships come quickly to mind, and there are agreed upon, relatively straightforward measures with which to assess them. What is needed is more connections to both empirical and experiential variables believed to be part of the complex interaction of biological, psychological, and social influences that result in psychopathology.

Aside from the wish for more from such remarkable longitudinal studies, what do the results of these two studies contribute to our thinking about the depressed woman whose dilemma was briefly outlined above? First, I believe, is that our search for important connections must be as broad as possible. Recall that the efforts to consistently identify genetic variables involved in various psychopathologies have not, for the most part, been successful. In these two studies the importance of genetic factors became apparent only when their connections to experiential factors (childhood maltreatment and life stress) were identified. Is it reasonable, therefore, to formulate that once the patient's life stress became extreme (the death of her husband), her 5–HTT genotype played a role in the development of her major depression? Even if such a formulation is reasonable, does it have clinical utility? One stance on its utility involves the awareness that the 5–HTT gene is involved in serotonin metabolism, and, as a consequence, one might search with greater diligence for an effective antidepressant directly impacting serotonin metabolism.

Another contribution of these studies is that they provoke us to think about what might add to their helpfulness. If, for example, adult attachment status was measured, would it inform us as to what experiences in childhood or later buffered the deleterious impact of childhood maltreatment? What would the relationship be between buffering or healing relationships and the forms of 5—HTT? As one begins to consider the possible network of connections, it seems clear that the search to be helpful to this depressed woman not be restricted to antidepressants; it should also include psychotherapeutic explorations of relevant intrapsychic and relational variables.

The studies reaffirm for our profession the need to avoid reductionisms of any sort and to continue our collaborative efforts with patients to search out relevant connections. We need to continue to be the first citizens of contingency.

References

1. Pinsky, R. (1975). "Essay on Psychiatrists" in *Sadness and Happiness*. Princeton, N.J.:Princeton Univ. Press.
2. Caspi, A., McClay, J. Moffitt, T.E., et al (2002). "Role of Genotype in the Cycle of Violence in Maltreated Children," Science, 297:2, August, 851-845.
3. Caspi, A., Sugden, K. Moffitt, T.E., et al (2003). "Influence of Life Stress on Depression: Moderation by a Polymorphism in the 5—HTT Gene," Science, 301:18, July, 386-389.

August 2005

33

TO ERR IS HUMAN

The first several sessions had been filled with her anger at her husband for his emotional unavailability. When she began our third session with more of the same, I asked her quietly if we could look at what she might be doing that kept him at a distance. She looked away, grew silent, and began to cry. After what seemed like a long time, she responded, "You're like all the rest, you simply don't understand."

I thought that my confrontation had been premature; that I had grown impatient with her angry, victim orientation. After a short silence I responded, "Tell me how it feels when I fail to understand." We were then able to gradually move beyond her defensive anger and explore her long history of fears of abandonment. My question about her possible role in her husband's retreat had been an error (at least, in timing) and the acknowledgement of my failure to understand—a correction of sorts—had facilitated a deeper exploration.

They brought the tape of their attempts to learn more of exploratory conversation to the office. It was the fifth in a series of similar homework assignments, and this one was to involve sharing with each other experiences of vulnerability that did not involve their relationship.

She told the story of a childhood experience in which she was separated from her mother at a large shopping mall. She was five years old at the time and recalled with much anxiety the terror she had felt. He listened, encouraging her to continue. As she became more anxious, however, he took over the conversation with a series of focused questions about the facts; about how she was reunited with her mother. She answered briefly and they terminated the conversation.

I turned off the tape and asked them what they had heard. He said, "I blew it. As she began to feel those frightening feelings, I turned her off by switching to the facts." She smiled slightly and nodded her agreement. I then asked them what they could have done differently. He said he could have recognized what he was doing, stopped it, and returned to her feelings. "What might you have done?" I asked her "I'm not sure," she responded. I suggested she, too, could have initiated the correction by telling him that he had moved away from where she was.

Some years ago I saw a research microbiologist who had writer's block. He apparently did excellent work and had no trouble analyzing his data. Writing it up and submitting papers for publication, however, were a terrible problem for him. He came in for a session and was unusually quiet. After 15 or 20 minutes, he told me—with much anxiety—that in the prior session I had completely missed the importance of what he had said. After exploring the details of how I had failed to understand, we turned to how difficult it was for him to confront me with my error. This piece of the exploration led to the uncovering of some of the key dynamics of his writer's block. It was an important turning point in his therapy.

These three psychotherapeutic experiences involving empathic failures and the importance of recognizing and correcting them are used to introduce one perspective regarding how interpersonal relationships may facilitate individual personality maturation.

Although much of contemporary developmental theory emphasizes that individual maturation occurs through the process of taking into oneself the admirable qualities of important others, there is little known about the mechanisms of such internalizations. Much of psychoanalytic theory suggests that it is the threatened loss of the important other that is crucial. Internalization is understood as the effort to prevent the loss. In a recent publication I have reviewed the emerging data that suggests that internalization occurs when a strong affective bond is disrupted and, most importantly, the disruption is repaired (1). From this perspective internalization is encouraged when the loss is prevented by the repair. Indeed, it seems reasonable to suggest that internalizations growing out of repetitive small losses (failure to repair disruptions) may lead to insecure (anxiety-filled) attachments rather than maturation.

The importance of the affective bond-disruption-repair sequence can be noted in the literature describing the three dyadic relations most often associated with individual growth. The initial impetus for this perspective comes from research on early infant-mother interactions. Tronick and his collaborators studied such interactions using slow motion photography and demonstrated that mothers were correctly attuned to their infants' signals only about one third of the time (2,3). When a maternal misattunement occurred, however, the infant communicated distress and, in an additional one third, the mothers made a successful correction. Infant-mother interactions do not demonstrate a stable synchrony; rather, misattunement and repair is an important process in establishing a secure attachment.

The importance of the therapeutic alliance in psychotherapy has been documented by studies indicating that the alliance may account for up to 50 percent of the variance in psychotherapeutic outcome (4). Safran has explored the determinants of an effective alliance by analyzing the verbatim transcripts of psychotherapy sessions (5). His data indicate that the therapists' ability to recognize and explore their errors is the most powerful predictor of an effective alliance. His work suggests that the exploration needs to focus on the patient's feelings about the therapist's error, and that the error needs to be openly acknowledged.

Marital therapists have long focused on couples not communicating clearly and the need to correct the resulting misunderstandings. The therapist helps the partners to clarify their feelings, to explore their individual subjective realities, and in being both open with and respectful of their differences. Misattunements and empathic failures lead to conflict and alienation: repairs encourage psychological intimacy. The study of marriages that facilitate individual maturation demonstrates that such couples have developed ways of communicating that increase the likelihood that when misattunements occur—as they inevitably do—repairs will sometimes occur.

It thus appears that in three of the dyadic relationships commonly associated with individual maturation (infant-mother, marital, and patient-therapist) there is increasing evidence that the corrections of errors in the form of misattunements, misunderstandings, ill-timed responses, and the like play a crucial role in solidifying the affective bond and, perhaps, over time setting the stage for growth-facilitating internalizations.

The problem this poses starts with recognizing one's errors. This may be easier with a spouse because partners learn each other's signals of misattunement. As a supervisor of individual psychotherapy who has used audiotapes of supervisees' psychotherapy sessions, however, I am impressed with how infrequently errors are recognized by therapists until they are pointed out in supervision. I also wonder how often in my own psychotherapeutic work I overlook or deny my errors unless the patient is able to communicate his or her disappointment in ways that are crystal clear.

It is 50 years since I started my residency, and it is obvious that the learning never stops. Indeed, one of the advantages of being a psychotherapist is the opportunity to continue learning about one's self and the inevitable errors one makes in "being there" for important others. Accepting the idea that "to err is human" and making the effort to acknowledge, explore, and correct the errors may be far more important that most of us have realized. It may, in fact, contribute to the building of relationships that encourage individual maturation.

References

1. Lewis J.M. (2000). "Repairing the Bond in Important Relationships: A Dynamic for Personality Maturation." Am J Psychiatry 157:9, 1375-1378, September.
2. Tronick E.Z., Gianino A. (1986). "Zero to three." Bulletin of the National Center for Clinical Infant Programs, 6:3, 1-6.
3, Tronick E., Als, H., Adamson L., Wise S., Brazelton B. (1978). "The Infant's Response to Entrapment Between Contradictory Messages in Face-to-Face Interaction." J Am Acad Child Psychiatry 17, 1-13.
4. Horvath A.O., Luborsky L. (1993). "The Role of the Therapeutic Alliance in Psychotherapy." J Consult Clin Psychol, 68, 651-673.
5. Safran J.D., McMain S., Crocker P., Murray P. (1990). "Therapeutic Alliance Rupture as a Therapy Event for Empirical Investigation." Psychotherapy, 27, 154-165.

November 2002

34

LEARNING THE PSYCHOTHERAPEUTIC PROCESS

The patient was finishing a lengthy recollection of a childhood experience in which her parents left her alone to go out drinking. A storm flew in and she was very frightened. "It was very bad," she said, "very, very scary."

The resident-therapist asked, "How long were they gone?" A long silence followed, and, finally, I suggested that we turn off the tape. After she had done so I asked her, "Why do you think you asked that question?"

The discussion that followed touched on how she (the resident) might feel if in recalling a very frightening experience the other person had not addressed her fear but had asked—more or less matter-of-factly—a temporal question. We talked about how one comes to feel understood, the ubiquitousness of separation anxiety, and how hard it was sometimes to listen to recollections from patients that provoked recall of one's own frightening experiences.

In all the years of supervising residents' psychotherapeutic efforts and those of practicing clinicians, I have suggested listening to audiotapes of their psychotherapy sessions. The tapes are remarkably illuminating. Most often they are filled with the resident's focused questions rather than flowing from the patient's narrative. Topic changes by the resident are frequent; response to obvious affective messages rare, interruption all too often, and interpretive comments freely given. In short, the resident does not seem to understand the key processes involved in psychotherapeutic work.

In listening to the tapes the memories of my experiences as a resident therapist come painfully back to mind. I was told to meet my new patient in the waiting room, take him or her to my clinic office, and "do" therapy. Later I was to discuss the session with my supervisor, in those days at Penn invariably a psychoanalyst or senior analytic candidate. The problem was that I had not idea of what "doing" psychotherapy was about. As a consequence, I began taking a detailed history. As part of that process, I asked multiple focused questions, was pleased with brief answers, and generally avoided affect.

The problems occurred later. The problem I was aware of was what do you do after you've taken the patient's history? The problem I was not aware of at the time was that my imposition of a directive structure on the initial encounters clearly implied that I was in charge of the relationship and, therefore perhaps responsible for the outcome.

After my residency it took me several years of listening to my psychotherapy tapes and studying the few tapes or transcripts of notable therapist then available to begin to understand something about psychotherapeutic process. Having some sense that, if one doesn't know very much about a subject, the best think to do is teach it. I began a seminar on psychotherapeutic process for residents. Later I took another step to advance my learning: I wrote several books about my experiences in teaching psychotherapeutic process (1,2).

Although my primary intent here is to outline briefly several aspects of psychotherapeutic process that need to be mastered by residents and young therapists, several caveats may be in order. First is the question of what kind of psychotherapy I am talking about. My answer is that I am talking about crucial relationship processes designed to establish an effective and collaborative therapeutic appliance to explore as thoroughly as possible the patient's subjective reality, and to come to a tentative, understanding of the patient's dilemma. Thus, I am talking about a generic model that I believe should be learned before the more specific techniques associated with different types of psychotherapy (psychoanalytic, cognitive, etc.) are learned.

A second caveat is that I am aware (but shall not cite) some of those few colleagues involved in teaching psychotherapeutic process to residents and/or clinical psychology graduate students. My admiration for their efforts during this period of dominance of a neuroscientific paradigm is boundless.

So, what needs to be learned? The key issue is learning how to facilitate the patient's story in order to experience and potentially understand the patient's narrative identity. At its core this involves both encouraging the patient's spontaneous narrative flow with as little interference as possible. Two major interventions are crucial. The first is the use of simple encouragers such as "Go on," "How interesting," "Tell me more," and the like. These encouragers do not direct the patient's narrative in this or that direction; rather they encourage the patient continuing in whatever direction his or her associations take the narrative. The second intervention involves attending particularly to the patient's affective messages and responding empathically. Examples are: "That must have hurt," "You felt utterly lost", or "It is very painful." Such responses have been demonstrated to encourage narrative flow.

That which is to be minimized are focused questions that suggest to the patient where the therapist believes the interview should go. It is also clear that nothing stops another's narrative flow as quickly as direct or implied judgmental statements ("You really didn't do that, did you?")

This type of conversation can be called "exploratory" in contrast to the more directive process involved in history-taking or, in an extreme form, the legal cross examination. The explanatory process is not aimed to arrive at a categorical diagnosis. If the context demands a categorical diagnosis and a series of direct, focused questions about the presence or absence of symptoms is necessary, some sort of bridging statement is needed. ("This is all interesting and very relevant, but I need now to change things temporarily and ask you a few direct questions.") Such statements announce the beginning of a directive process in which the clinician takes over the interview process—thus switching from a more collaborative, patient-centered process to one in which the therapist assumes control.

My teaching experiences suggest that a directive conversational style is ingrained in medical students as well as other young professionals. The task is to teach a second type of conversation style, and that the context should determine which type is more appropriate. I shared with students one night long ago when I had accidentally injured a nerve to my chest, began splinting my chest movements, and developed a collapsed lung and plural effusion. I was in severe pain and, in retrospect, was grateful that my internist-friend-neighbor used a brief directive conversational style rather than an exploratory one. We got to the emergency room and hospitalization quickly. The context demanded a directive conversation.

Students usually have real problems learning to use an exploratory conversational style. When uncertain about how to respond, they invariably revert to a directive style by asking a series of focused questions. Years ago, one seminar student put her finger to a major source of anxiety when she reflected, "It's kind of scary not knowing where the conversation is going. With direct questions I feel in charge of what the patient and I are going to talk about." Such anxiety has to be validated but also compensated for by the suggestion that part of the satisfaction of psychotherapeutic work is that of new and often surprising adventures. "It never gets told or boring if each patient provides you with the possibility of a new adventure," I am apt to say.

I wish I had been offered such learning experiences as a resident. Senior colleagues have often expressed the same wish. More than such subjective responses, however, there is some suggestion in the psychotherapy outcome research that the therapeutic alliance accounts for a large proportion of the outcome variable. An effective alliance is more likely when the therapist shows respect for the patient's subjective reality, demonstrates empathy for the patient's predicament, works collaboratively, and corrects his or her errors.

There are also data from the study of "healing" marriages that indicate that some of the same exploratory processes are used in some circumstances by marital partners (3). Shared power, respect for subjective reality, and exploratory conversations appear to strengthen the emotional bond between the partners.

Thus, one avenue of healing processes may be conversational in that it grows out of feeling safe in exposing vulnerabilities and trusting that the feedback will be respectful.

In these days of reduced time and effort devoted to psychotherapy in our training programs, it might be very helpful to not just mandate the time devoted to psychotherapy training but also to develop learning experiences that systematically teach beginners some of what is known about psychotherapeutic process.

References

1. Lewis, J.M. (1978). *To Be a Therapist: The Teaching and Learning.* New York: Brunner-Mazel.
2. Lewis, J.M. (1991). *Swimming Upstream: Teaching and Learning Psychotherapy in a Biological Era.* New York: Brunner-Mazel.
3. Lewis, Jerry M. (1997). *Marriage As A Search For Healing.* New York: Brunner-Mazel.

March 2004

35

THERAPY WITH A FRIEND WITH DEMENTIA

He stared at me with an intensity that suggested something unusual. "What are those needles doing in your chest?" he asked. "What needles?," I responded, while feeling my chest. "Maybe little knives," he said. "I can't feel them," was my reply. He got out of his chair and felt my chest. "Damn," he exclaimed, "I saw them." "I wonder how they got there?" I asked softly. We went on to explore his repressed anger at me for a three-week interruption of our twice-weekly psychotherapy sessions during a period of teaching at a distant medical school.

I had known him as teacher, colleague, and friend for over 50 years. When his early dementia forced him to give up his psychotherapy practice, he became clinically depressed. He turned to me, and I told him he needed an antidepressant and psychotherapy. He agreed with the former but questioned the latter. We talked about it, and, at length he agreed. His contingency was that I be his therapist. I refused, citing our long friendship, and he insisted, pointing out that the therapy he needed was not going to require exploration and resolution of the transference. Further, I was the only psychotherapist he would agree to see. We remained stalemated for days, but ultimately I agreed to see him but without a fee. He resisted this strenuously, but I remained firm. Why I agreed to be his psychotherapist almost certainly involved a number of factors. At a conscious level the more I thought about it and discussed it with my wife, the more "right" it seemed to be. Only later did I recall Kleinman's comment (in discussing patients with chronic diseases) that empathic witnessing is a moral act rather than a technical procedure (1).

Thus we began what turned out to be twice weekly sessions in his home that lasted for 18 months at which time his increasing dementia precluded conversational interchanges. For the next several years and until his death I went by weekly to sit quietly with him and support his wife and the remarkable care she gave him.

In this column the focus will not be on seeing a friend in psychotherapy and whether there are particular circumstances in which such is in the patient-friend's best interest. Rather, my intent is to share the experience of psychotherapy with a patient with progressive dementia, a psychotherapy that came to focus on his experience of the dementia and the gradual loss of his usual sense of self.

The psychotherapy, however, did not begin as an effort to deal with his dementia; rather it was an effort to help him deal with his loss of professional identity and subsequent depression. The focus of each interview, beginning with my customary opening, "How do you feel?", was wherever he took us. An early focus on his childhood experiences, for example, grew out of his statement, "You probably need to know about my childhood." Over the course of many interviews we established that his defining conflictual childhood relationship was with his unaffectionate, hardworking, and demanding father. His response was to be compliant, a "good boy," and this identity had persisted. Being a good boy was understood as a factor in much of his very real success in his roles of physician, psychotherapist, husband, father, and friend. Its cost, however, was his need to repress anger even in those circumstances in which anger seemed appropriate. Hence when his dementia came to involve occasional hallucinations he needed to project his unacceptable anger at me as knives in my chest.

The focus on his experience of dementia arose on those occasions when he could not remember or got lost in the middle of a sentence. If he showed no distress on those occasions, I did not comment. If, however, he became anxious, I would comment with reflections like, "It is hard to lose your way." He would respond sometimes by changing the subject, but other times clearly indicated a wish to explore these symptoms.

Out of such explorations a major dilemma was identified. To face his dementia was experienced with much anxiety. We came to call this position, "Fighting the Dragon." However, to deny consistently his increasingly apparent symptoms ("Floating Down the River"), came to be experienced as a loss of his usual sense of self. He complained that he had never experienced himself as either avoidant or passive, and that doing so regarding his symptoms made him very anxious. Thus, to struggle directly with his symptoms was filled with anxiety but to deny them also led to anxiety. My responses to this final conflict was to try to be accurately empathic. No resolution was really possible. "The only solution," he said sadly, "is sleep, and I'm doing a lot of that."

He remained remarkably himself during the 18 months of psychotherapy. His mood remained mostly euthymic. Until the end he was curious, open, and clearly invested in our sessions. "Is this a day Jerry is coming?" he asked his wife most mornings. True to his good boy identity, he never expressed anger at his fate.

As indicated earlier, I did not begin this psychotherapy with a friend with the intent of helping him deal with his dementia. In addition, I was not conversant with the emerging literature on the psychological dimensions of treating demented patients. I did have the somewhat vague notion that dominant treatment approaches did not advise directly addressing the dementia symptoms. Thus, I was neither directed nor hindered by the opinions of experts.

My earlier work with dying friends had taught me that they invested intensely in our work together (2). I came to believe that what helped was the presence of an empathic other that diminished their experience of aloneness. To face death, the existentialists remind us, is to face profound anxiety. To face death alone adds to that anxiety for many. My experience with my demented friend appears, I believe, to involve the same process. I was able to be "with him" as he struggled with his final dilemma—how best to deal with his dementia and, at the same time, maintain as much of his usual sense of self as possible.

I do not know how generalizable this psychotherapeutic experience is. My friend was a psychotherapist, and the psychotherapy context was comfortable for him. Self-awareness was an important value for him. At the same time, it is not difficult to wonder whether there are other persons for whom an exploratory, empathic approach would be helpful.

The psychotherapeutic work with my friend had its personal costs and benefits. I was often sad about losing an important friend. My occasional memory problems (particularly with names of persons and objects) became a source of more-than-usual anxiety. At the same time, my friend taught me much about courage; about dealing with an insolvable dilemma by trying to face it; about struggling to retain the usual sense of self under the most trying of circumstances. Our work together also forced me to again deal with my own internal contradictions. I am old but wish to experience myself as young and vital. I can be effective, but also helpless. These and other contradictions were often in my thoughts after our sessions.

Like most psychotherapeutic encounters, the exchange seemed equal. I believe our work together was helpful to both of us.

References

1. Kleinman, A. (1988). *The Illness Narratives: Suffering, Healing, and the Human Condition.* New York: Basic Books.
2. Lewis, J.M. (1982). "Dying With Friends: Implications for the Psychotherapist." American Journal of Psychiatry, March.

November 2003

36

USING EXISTENTIAL CONCEPTS IN PSYCHOTHERAPY

A 60 year-old surgeon was seen with complaints of depressed mood, sleep disturbance, and anorexia. He described three failed marriages, alienation from his two grown children, and no close friends. His account of his childhood experiences involved an emotionally distant mother and absent father. He described himself as a compliant person who valued clear structure, absolute rules, and dedication to his patients. It seemed clear that he was a constricted, compulsive person whose major depression had developed following his divorce from his third wife. He was not religious and, during the initial interview, reflected that he had been a distant and unsuccessful husband, a poor father, and his only sense of personal meaning had involved being a good surgeon. And, now, he could see looming the end of his surgical practice.

His internist had prescribed several antidepressants and pushed their dosages to the limit without, however, any clear effect upon his symptoms. Thus, the referral to me.

After several exploratory interviews, it became obvious that I had to select a theoretical perspective from which to treat him. In this deliberation the work of Havens on the Schools of psychiatry provided a systematic approach (1). Havens described four schools—the objective-descriptive, the psychoanalytic, the interpersonal, and the existential.

When viewed from the objective-descriptive perspective my focus would be on his major depression and compulsive personality traits. Treatment would most likely involve a systematic search for an effective antidepressant (or combination thereof). He would be understood as a person with an illness—an illness that had a life of its own at some distance from his personhood.

A psychoanalytic perspective would lead to psychotherapy with a major focus on his experience of loss, his mechanisms of defense against the emergence of long repressed affects, and the attempt to manage the likely development of a negative (hostile, retreating) transference and a negative (boredom, exasperation) countertransference. This perspective would deal with his major depression as a distinct and understandable part of his personhood.

The interpersonal perspective would focus on his interpersonal relationships and his failure to achieve a lasting intimacy. It would focus on his defensive need to avoid vulnerability by keeping others at great emotional distance. If he had come to me before his third divorce, some consideration would have been given to treating him in a couples therapy context because that format can involve a more direct approach to intimacy problems (2). The interpersonal approach, however, is a clearly described manner of conducting individual psychotherapy. It's focus is on the person's transactions with important others and/or the relational self.

The existential approach to this man's dilemma would interpret his depression as a manifestation of an existential crises involving the lack of meaning in his life. Having found no source of personal meaning in either God or love, he relied only on his efficacy as a surgeon, and that slender need of meaning was about to disappear. As Havens pointed out, the existential school of psychiatry is the least attended to in this country, and although its focus may be considered the very essence of this man's personhood.

My reading of current psychotherapeutic practice is that most therapists use an eclectic mix of these four perspectives. It seems likely that this depressed physician would be treated with further attempts to find an effective combination of antidepressant drugs and some form of psychotherapy (psychodynamic, cognitive, or interpersonal). What seems most certain is that there is but a slight possibility of his treatment being influenced by an existential perspective.

Another possibility is the selection of a treatment perspective that appears to best fit the circumstances of the individual patient. Perhaps in part because aging therapists like me think frequently of their own existential dilemmas, but, also because my patient's presentation appeared clearly to raise existential issues, the existential perspective was chosen. I told him that if our work together was not helpful we would ask a psychiatrist-expert in polypharmacy to consult.

Although there is no broadly accepted existential model of psychological functioning, Yalom's work has been for me remarkably helpful(3). His discussion of the four basic "ultimate concerns" (meaningfulness, death, responsibility, and isolation)n as the most basic of all psychological structures combined with a strong emphasis on therapist empathy has guided me when such an approach seemed to best fit the patient's situation.

We began our work with what seemed to be most troubling to him—his aloneness. This theme ran through all his early memories, his dreams, and, of course, his current life situation. He was able to get in touch with how knowing his wives were in the same house at night—even thought there were only a few actual interactions—comforted him. Although his relationships with his office staff seemed formal and distant, he felt better when he was in the office with them. His nights and weekends were filled with loneliness.

After a number of sessions with this focus on the pain of his isolation, a second theme arose; that of his responsibility for his aloneness (the ultimate concern of freedom or groundlessness). He explored his almost total failure to reach out to others and the feared vulnerability that was so much a part of his distancing.

Later he began to ask himself if there was something he could do about his isolation—however tentative and faltering such efforts might be. He wondered about trying to return to the church of his childhood, volunteering as a member of a physician group at a local homeless shelter, going to medical meetings, and even joining a singles group. These activities were filled with anticipatory anxiety, and he asked for my recommendations. After responding empathically to his anxiety, I responded, "You must make the decision and take the responsibility for the consequences of going or not going."

He also explored the issue of his life's meaning and appeared to conclude that his greatest opportunity to develop a greater sense of meaning was through relationships, particularly those that involved giving more of himself to others. He loved classical music, for example, but had never volunteered to serve the local symphony.

Through all of his work with me, I tried to maximize the empathic component of psychotherapy and to avoid directiveness and the giving of much requested support. His response was clearly ambivalent. I was both the empathic parent and the frustrating object who would not take over his life and provide him with a new structure. He expressed the positive affect directly: "I've never been able to talk with anyone like we talk." The negative affect was clear in his dreams wherein a parental figure never loved him enough.

His depressive symptomatology gradually cleared. He began to experiment cautiously with reaching out by joining the physician volunteers two afternoons a week, at the homeless center. A little later he started dating a widowed woman physician on the hospital staff. These activities were filled with anxiety which he brought into therapy. After 14 months of mostly once-a-week psychotherapy he suggested an every two week format. As I write this it is four years since we began our work together and he calls for an appointment several times a year. He has remained free of depressive symptomatology and remarried. In his relationship with his new wife he reports trying hard and with some success to be more available to her, more sensitive to her needs, and more openly affectionate. "It is not easy for me" he reported, "but it is surprising how responsive she is to my efforts. I feel less alone—more connected than ever before."

The issue of how our work together was helpful to him in emerging from a major depression and becoming, I believe, somewhat less distancing is impossible to answer with certainty. Did it have anything to do with our shared focus on his ultimate concerns? Was it due to the strong working alliance we jointly constructed? Has it involved the internalization of an empathic other? What role did new insights play? These and other questions address the unknowns clinicians struggle with in the attempt to understand psychotherapeutic outcomes.

Despite our collective inability to know precisely what helps, the outcome of the patients and joint psychotherapeutic effort was successful. I'd like to believe that it had something to do with the existential perspective used because it seemed to fit his initial definition of his dilemma. Ah, well, isn't that uncertainty a part of the fascination of being a psychotherapist?

References

1. Havens, L.L. (1973). *Approaches to the Mind.* Boston: Little, Brown, & Co.
2. Lewis, J.M. (1997). *Marriage as a Search for Healing: Theory, Assessment, and Therapy.* New York: Brunner-Mazel.
3. Yalom, I. D. (1980). *Existential Psychotherapy.* New York: Boston Books, Inc.

January 2004

37

DYING WITH FRIENDS REVISITED

His dying was slow and, although not painful, involved profound weakness. He could not get out of bed or walk even a few steps without help. The weakness was especially difficult because his sense of self had always been that of a strong person, a decision-maker, and leader of important public agencies and professional organizations. In our talks he was clear that this quality of life was no longer tolerable: he wanted it to end. And, yet, he did not want to leave his wife and family. This final conflict—wanting and not wanting to die—was explored over and over again without, of course, resolution. I tried only to let him know that I could feel the pain with him—that he did not have to be entirely alone with it.

This experience with a dying friend is one of eight that I have encountered. Each of the eight were psychotherapists and most asked to see me—usually in tentative, indirect ways—shortly after learning of their terminal illnesses. I spent a few hours with several and more than 100 hours with others. Although the experience outlined above was with a close friend, most of the others did not involve a preexisting intimate friendship. Some years ago the experiences with the first four dying friends were published (1). The purpose of this column is to revisit the experience of being with dying friends and to suggest several implications for clinical practice.

One common feature was that in the context of a nondirective conversational format a final theme gradually evolved. This theme often took the form of a conflict. The wish to die and yet not experience separation from loved ones was most common. This may have been influenced in part by the fact that none of the dying psychotherapists appeared to believe in an afterlife and reunion with loved ones. It also speaks to the ubiquitousness of separation anxiety, and the existentialist premise that aloneness is one of the ultimate concerns.

Other final themes took the form of regrets rather than conflicts. A male psychiatrist, for example, needed to talk about what he considered his greatest failure, the inability to sustain a committed relationship with a woman. "I think I've been a good father and a capable therapist," he said, "but I have never been able to have a lasting love relationship. I totally failed to give my three wives what they needed, and, with all that I think I know about myself, I didn't change that pattern."

Another psychotherapist talked about his regret about always being a "good boy." "All my life I've done what I thought I ought to do and sacrificed what I wanted to do. Even this terribly deforming cancer surgery—I agreed to it in order to be a good patient. I fell in love years ago but couldn't either leave my unhappy marriage or have an affair. Good boys don't do such things, and now I think I missed so much."

Another final theme involved the fear that dying would be so painful or frightening that one's usual sense of self would be lost. One man talked about the fear that he would turn into "a crying baby." A woman feared the loss of control that had characterized her sense of self. Both of these friends asked me if I would help them die if their dying overwhelmed them. Neither asked for that help, but they needed to hear an affirmative response. I don't know what I would have done if they had asked, but I did discuss their situations and asked for advice from my county medical society.

Having someone to discuss these final themes with became very important to these dying friends. They looked forward to our visits and often requested greater frequency as the end neared. I have wondered why I was selected to be with these friends in their dying. Although multiple factors were likely involved, one that seems important is separation anxiety. Leaving me was not nearly as painful as separating from spouses and others they loved.

One implication is clear. The opportunity to have someone share the experience of dying means not to be alone with it. In a situation in which there was literally nothing active I could do, empathy was all that could be offered. There are clinical situations other than dying in which the therapist's empathy is crucial. I have seen patients with Crohn's Disease, dementing processes, and other progressive diseases in which the issue of adaptation to suffering began when patients felt not alone. Although the psychotherapy outcome research suggests that empathy is a necessary but insufficient condition for successful outcome, that should not blind us to its often crucial importance when patients are facing insolvable dilemmas.

Another implication is also clear: To be with someone who is facing an insolvable dilemma has its cost. Being with dying friends was painful for me. I tended to deny the pain at the time despite my wife's gentle confrontations that I seemed preoccupied, unavailable, perhaps depressed. On one occasion I acted out the wish to avoid my pain by driving to the wrong hospital—despite having been to the right hospital many times. Generally it was only some time after the dying friends had died that I felt more myself and better able to accept my wife's accurate perceptions.

Several themes emerged in my dreams. One involved my own death. When was it coming? What form would it take? How would I deal with it? I often found myself admiring the ways in which these friends were dying. On several occasions I said something like, "I really admire the way you are handling this dying business, and hope I can do as well when it's my turn."

Another theme involved helplessness. This more conscious affect contradicted my usual sense of being an active problem-solver, a person who could get things done. Despite the realization that I was being helpful, these experiences led me to face the internal contradiction between feeling powerful and feeling helpless. At some level I apparently believed I should be able to do more. A psychoanalyst who I saw while he was dying helped me face this internal contradiction when he smilingly reported his dreams that I had discovered a cure for his terminal pulmonary disease.

All of these painful experiences led to new insights about myself.

Getting in closer touch with my own separation anxiety was one. Others involved clarifying my internal contradictions such as young —old, powerful—helpless, and self-preoccupied—altruistic. Still others involved greater awareness of my mechanisms of defense, some of them not all that mature.

Thus, the time, energy, and pain involved was counterbalanced by that which my work with dying friends did for me. Their gratitude and that of their families is balanced by my gratitude for what their dying taught me about me.

Reference

1. Lewis, J.M. (1982). "Dying With Friends: Implications for the Psychotherapist," Am J Psych, 139:3, 261-266.

March 2003

38

STEPPING ON THE OXYGEN TUBE

He was a therapist and friend who was dying of metastatic cancer. When he asked if we could talk, I began to go by his hospital room, ultimately spending an hour or so with him at the end of each day. During over 30 such visits we talked about many things—his wife and family, his career, and, at times his dying. I tried only to be there, to be with him in a way that gave him some relief from his aloneness (1).

Courage was an important theme in his life. He was a decorated veteran of Pacific Island invasions in World War II and an outspoken public speaker on current social injustices. I knew this about him and as death became imminent his anxiety about losing control and "becoming a baby" became obvious. Several days before he died he asked me if it got too much for him would I step on his oxygen tube? Without a moment's thought I said, "Yes." Such was not necessary as he lapsed into coma and died a day later.

The other occasion in which I was asked if I would help if dying became too difficult was also some years ago. This situation developed in the context of a doctor-patient relationship. I had seen this middle-aged woman and her husband in couples therapy six years earlier, and our work together had been successful. She called and asked if I could help with her dying as much as I had helped with her living. She, too, had metastatic cancer.

During the six months she lived I saw her and her husband weekly, alternating individual sessions with couples work. She had been the more distant, analytic spouse whose difficulty with intimacy appeared related to childhood experiences with what sounded like a chronically depressed mother, herself a Holocaust survivor.

About a month before she died and during a session that included her husband she asked if dying became too miserable would I help her with it? Again, my response was immediate, "Of course," I said. I will not describe in detail the subsequent events—including my discussing the situation with the executive director of my local medical society and his suggestion that I talk with the recently retired pathologist-director of the medical examiner's office about how to help if that was my decision. For present purposes all that is relevant is that she never asked; rather she, too, slipped into a terminal coma.

I have thought often about these two situations, particularly in the context of the ongoing legal conflicts about Oregon's physician—assisted suicide law. What has particularly occupied my self-explorations has been the immediacy of my affirmative response to both my friend and my patient. Why—without any thoughts about the implications of what I was being asked to do—did I respond so quickly and emphatically?

One line of my thinking concerns the demands of the context. With both friend and patient in such dire circumstances, how could one have said, "no", or "maybe," or "we'll see?" The context demanded an affirmative response. The dying person needed to hear that help would be available if requested. My immediate and affirmative response reflected my understanding of that context and its demand quality.

I suspect that responding to the context played a role in my response, but there is almost certainly more to it than that. It is hard to avoid the conclusion that my underlying anxiety about my own death must have influenced my response. If my death were unusually painful wouldn't I want someone to slip me the requisite pills?

Death anxiety is considered by many existentialists to be an ultimate concern, one of the most fundamental processes in the entire psychology of the self. Becker, in his famous, *The Denial of Death,* proposed that it is the most basic font of all psychopathology, and that we defend vigorously against directly experiencing it (2). Subsequent research efforts have distinguished conscious death anxiety from unconscious death anxiety. The former is considered multifaceted. Some persons' conscious death anxiety involves separation from loved ones; for others it might be fear of the unknown; there are a handful of interrelated themes involved in conscious death anxiety. Unconscious death anxiety is, of course, more difficult to study. One approach uses a sentence completion format and demonstrates that there are clear distinctions between the two types of death anxiety (3).

Although I think consciously about my own death (after all, I am approaching 82) without severe conscious anxiety, some idea of the extent of my unconscious death anxiety was revealed to me some years ago when I said goodbye to my wife on the way to the operating room for major league surgery. So, I know it's there—and that it has to do, at least in part, with separation from her. Is it that deep dread within me that prompted my immediate responses? Is the idea of a prolonged and painful dying so frightening at an unconscious level to me that I leap to assuage those fears in others? This is a reasonable hypothesis, and I suspect it is part of the picture. I say this because my more usual behavior is far more cautious than impulsive, and my immediate and emphatic response to the request for help in dying is not at all typical.

A third theme probably operating in my responses was my underlying heroic aspirations. These aspirations may be fulfilled by rescuing a patient or friend from severe pain, hopelessness, and fear of dying. To rescue others has an unknown relationship to the need to be helpful, although as a resident, in a then psychoanalytic department of psychiatry, I learned that any hint of "rescue fantasies" was a neurotic trait. It was only after reading Becker's premise that heroic aspirations are ubiquitous and in the service of the search for immortality that the question (for me) came to be not whether one has heroic aspirations but how intense they are and whether they negate the needs of the others (2).

There is a fourth possible factor suggested, in part, by my behavior following my patient's request. My friend's death was so imminent that I doubted that he had enough conscious time left to ask me to step on his oxygen tube. Recall that after my patient's request I talked with authorities about the clinical situation and my assurance of help if needed. Without thinking about the implications of my response at the time, I knew, at some level, that I had the time to cover my rear. This sounds more like me.

These four possible explanations of my responses to these requests for help with dying may have all played a role. They are, however, not the whole story. What also seems clearly involved is my assumptive world (or values, belief system, etc.). I believe that a person has the right to determine his or her own death. Although this belief is heavily qualified by the research suggesting that some—perhaps 20 percent - of chronically ill persons also struggle with major depression and no longer wish to die if their depression is adequately treated. Once that qualification is dealt with I believe in the right to die on one's own terms.

My critics will say that I avoid the central issue: should physicians be allowed to assist in their patients' dying? Is this not a serious abandonment of the physician's healing role? Is it not the first step in the direction of the Nazi physicians' misuse of and killing of prisoners? Although I have mixed feelings about the pros and cons of this argument, in general I have thought that the domino theory is vastly overdone as a presumed powerful, more-or-less inevitable process in human systems. Earlier in this essay I described turning to a wise executive secretary of my medical society. We talked at length, but what I remember most of all, was his statement, "Jerry, all you must be certain of is that what you do is in the patient's best interests. That's what's right to do."

I do believe that my response to these two requests for possible help with dying were in the best interests of those dying persons. As I have tried to make clear in this essay, however, the nature of my responses also suggests that it is very likely that a number of personal unconscious processes combined to determine my responses. There are most likely other of my characteristics that also were involved, so I continue from time to time to try to sort it all out, provoked in part by the press reports of the government's attempted intrusion into what seems a highly complex matter between patient and doctor.

References

1. Lewis, J.M. (1982). "Dying With Friends: Implications for the Psychotherapist", Am J Psychiatry, 139:3, March.
2. Becker, E. (1973). *The Denial of Death.* New York: The Free Press.
3. Hayslip, Jr., B, et al (2001-02). "Death Anxiety: An Empirical Test of a Blended Self-Report and Projective Measurement Model." Omega, 44:3, 277-294.

July 2006

39

STRUGGLING WITH STALEMATES

There are occasions wherein one's best psychotherapeutic efforts are not effective or help only modestly. If the effort has taken place for a relatively long period of time, the therapist has several options. One is to ask a colleague for consultation. A second is to re-examine one's understanding of the patient's dilemma.

In this essay I will discuss some of the attempts to re-appraise my understanding of one type of such stalemates, that involving couples therapy with a severely conflicted couple. In the past several decades this situation has occurred in a handful of such couples.

They were both in their mid-thirties and had been married twelve years. Each was attractive and articulate. Both were also successful, she as a media consultant and he as a law school professor. They were also both independent and strongly opinioned. Each had experienced significant childhood trauma, she at the hands of an alcoholic father and a mother unable to protect her sufficiently, and he as a victim of parental discord and divorce who had been sent to live with grandparents where he experienced severe loneliness.

Their relationship had been conflicted from the start. Several weeks of truce (during which they enjoyed similar interests) were followed by a raging conflict with angry blaming of each other terminated by either emotional retreat (hours or days of silence) or one of them actually leaving for some hours. Threats of divorce were not uncommon but never acted upon. Each was in individual therapy which seemed helpful in their developing deeper understandings of themselves, but their intensely conflicted relationship pattern was mostly unchanged.

In my several years of work with them as a couple, there was but modest progress. The frequency and intensity of their periods of conflict were moderated, and, at times, they could listen respectfully to each other. In my office, however, it was rare for conflict not to erupt. When it did the affect was intense and the blaming pervasive. These uncomfortable periods were often difficult to interrupt—my taking a very directive stance most often resulted in only a momentary cessation.

As the sessions went on it became impossible not to be impressed by the stereotyped nature of their conflict. Although the content of each clash differed from episode to episode, the sequences of their behaviors were entirely predictable. Blaming and escalation were the rule. Even their changes in postures were coordinated as closely as the movements of experienced dancers moving toward and away from each other.

My mostly ineffectual efforts to help them change their destructive relationship pattern included a wide variety of interventions ranging from behavioral prescriptions to psychoeducational tactics to interpretive suggestions (1). They were faithful in keeping their appointments and doing their homework assignments, but the basic conflictual pattern persisted. On several occasions I suggested a consultation or that another therapist with a different approach might be a helpful direction in which to move. They demurred saying that they trusted me and, despite the stalemated situation, wished to continue with me.

Under such stalemated conditions the therapist needs to reexamine his or her understanding of the relational dynamics in play. More specifically, what underlying purpose is served by the repetitive, stereotyped conflictual interaction pattern that, at a very different level, requires a type of subtle cooperative behavior from both? It is in this sense that they can be understood as colluding in the repetition of a jointly constructed and clearly painful dance.

In the search to better understand the interactional pattern and the failure of treatment interventions to do anything but partially modify it, the problem is which theoretical lens offers the most promise. The more-or-less standard lens, that of systems theory, suggests that anger and conflict produce emotional distance—a distance that protects each participant from his and her underlying fears of dangerous (but desired) intimacy. When both partners have such fears they are likely to collude in periods of distance-producing conflict. This way of understanding this couple is a coherent way of looking at their dilemma, but my interventions based on making closeness less dangerous had not been successful.

A second theoretical lens is derived from psychoanalytic theory and emphasizes their shared use of projective identification. In this format the focus is on each partner's unconscious projection to the other of undesirable characteristics within the self and then behaving in ways that encourage the partner to respond or "act out" the undesirable projection. Although shared projective identifications may serve diverse purposes (including, of course, ridding the individual of unwanted aspects of the self), at the relational level, I believe, they are designed to produce predictability. In a world filled with uncertainty and randomness and with a personal history of injury from early caretakers, creating a predictable response from one's partner—however painful—can be experienced as safety. At the very least, knowing what is going to happen next, knowing at some level that one can produce a highly predictable response from the other can mean one has some control in a dangerous interpersonal world.

Although I believe that reciprocal projective identifications is a valid way of understanding this couple's relational dynamics, it, too, has not led to impactful interventions.

A third theoretical lens emphasizes existential constructs. The collusive, stereotyped pattern of conflict is understood as allowing each partner to avoid deeper anxiety stemming from existential ultimate concerns. In particular the pattern allows them to avoid facing the concern of existential isolation, or feeling all alone in the world. In this approach to their interactional pattern each partner avoids the anxiety about being without a central relationship that buffers (somewhat) the dread of isolation "However fleeting there are moments when I feel less alone", is one way to frame the issue. One sees couples who remain in chronically conflicted relationships and are aware that they stay because there are such moments.

Once again, this interpretive lens brings possible understanding, but its usefulness has been limited.

In using as examples these three interpretive lenses I am clearly avoiding the obvious. I have become an important part of their system. They give numerous examples of this: "What would Lewis say?" "What has Lewis taught us to try when we find ourselves beginning to behave this way?" "How is Lewis going to help us rescript this episode?" These questions only touch the surface of the fact that I am now part of the problem. Although I find each of them very likeable as individuals, their co-constructed relationship mostly defies my efforts to be helpful to them. Much of their continuing pattern may involve their reaction to an authoritative parental figure, a presumed expert whose power must be unconsciously negated even if the price is the continuance of a mutually destructive relationship pattern. In such a scenario I begin to feel the helplessness that, in part, disarms me, and they defend against their shared fears of what happens in an interpersonal system in which a parental figure has more power than one has.

This interpretive lens involves both the reality of my approach to couples therapy (I am often authoritative) and their transference fears. They do not retreat from therapy; it continues to be an important source of hope for them. At the same time their shared, fear-based resistance to change facilitates the continuance of the status quo.

As I hope has been made clear, psychotherapists need to have multiple theoretical lenses available to them and search for that which offers to have the greatest utility. Usefulness triumphs truth. Stalemates are particularly effective teachers of that lesson.

Reference

1. Lewis, J.M. (1997). *Marriage as a Search for Healing: Theory, Assessment and Therapy.* New York: Brunner-Mazel.

August 2007

40

MOMENTS OF REVELATION

There are moments in therapy that seem to have a special, illuminative quality; something important is suddenly revealed. Such moments may come as the result of deliberate observational and interventional processes or emerge from the therapist's unconscious. Either way, however, there is the sense that something important has been experienced. During a recent week I had two such experiences, making me wonder if I wasn't somehow more turned on those several days, more sensitive than usual. Since both of the experiences took place during initial interviews, one with a couple and the other with an individual, I did not have to struggle with the usual doubts about having missed the obvious in previous sessions.

The couple came at the advice of their rabbi and as part of a series of premarital procedures. They were both in their 50s and shared histories of dysfunctional childhood families and adult relationship failures. Each was a successful professional—she a doctoral level teacher in a local community college and he a pathologist at a nearby teaching hospital. They had been together for three years, the last of which involved living together. He seemed deliberate and cautious; she was full of affect. At about the midpoint of an initial 90-minute interview he described his only sibling, a younger brother, as a successful businessman. She responded by softly disagreeing with him.

"Jim," she said, "Your brother has had real difficulties holding on to jobs for more than a year or so."

He was silent for a few moments and then (with much emphasis), said "He *is* a successful businessman."

She looked away, the animation drawn from her face. The tense silence grew until he went on to describe other aspects of his family experiences. After several minutes I asked them if either was aware of what had happened between them a few moments ago. They were both silent—she with what I thought was a sad expression and he looking perplexed. I said, "Here's what I observed. Jim, you were describing your brother as successful. Jane, you disagreed—pointing out his difficulty sticking with a job. Jim you repeated—with great emphasis—that your brother was successful. Then, Jane, you looked away and I thought your face looked sad."

They were silent for a moment, then Jane began to softly cry. "This is really a big issue for me. All my life I've struggled not to be dominated, to have my own voice—and as much as I love Jim—there are these moments when I feel totally unheard. It's as if I don't exist."

"And, yet, " I responded, "You said nothing—just turned away, sadly, I think."

"I'm too afraid," she said, "I'm afraid I'll lose him if I disagree too often with him."

"Jim," I said, "Are you aware of how absolute you can be—and what that does to Jane? She feels that she doesn't exist at that moment and then is too afraid to let you know how she feels."

"I am not aware of coming across in such absolute terms, but know it would bother me if someone very important to me talked that way to me. It's something I need to do something about," he responded.

We went on to discuss this central relationship dynamic and possible ways of dealing with it. They agreed that he was drawn to her affectivity and she to his solid, down-to-earth quality, and that, unless she could become more comfortably outspoken, and he more aware of his relational impact, trouble might be in their future.

The major point of this essay, however, is the illuminative quality of their brief interaction. It is as if they jointly opened a window on an important dimension of their relationship structure. This allowed me to explore the interaction with them, and the result was the beginning of new learning about dealing with differences, respect for each other's subjective reality, and the relational language of negotiation. This was made possible not by any special skill on my part but by following the rule (in dealing with couples or families) that the clinician's conscious focus should be more on patterns of interaction than on individual characteristics.

The second experience occurred with an older man who had flown in from a distant city for an afternoon consultation. His wife accompanied him and, although I spent some time with her and some time with them together, the bulk of my time was with him alone.

His story involved having accidentally run into his college sweetheart of many years ago. His wife was out of town at the time, and he felt increasingly preoccupied, perhaps obsessed, with the woman from his youth. They began to exchange messages and then arranged a several day visit together. Although nothing in a physical sense happened, his time with this woman came to have a special aura. He was excited and began to feel that his earlier love for her had been rekindled, and that he needed to spend a period of weeks, even several months with her in order to evaluate what to do. The problem, of course, was that such was unacceptable to his wife—doing so meant the end of their marriage.

The context of this clinical situation included the following. His present marriage was of 25 years duration and described as a major and positive turning point in his life. His past history included childhood neglect by his prominent parents and early adult relationship failures. It was this marriage that had been experienced as healing. Further, his wife's trip out of town (a fun trip with close women friends) had occurred right at the time of his 80th birthday. He denied anger about this, saying it had been planned for a long time.

His wife, in turn, reported that in the several months before his birthday he had been increasingly irritable, experiencing early morning awakening, and had been drinking more than usual.

As I was sorting out an initial formulation of his and their dilemma in order to offer some recommendations, my mind turned to the role of his repressed anger about her trip, his possible narcissistic issues (the usual rules do not apply—I should have my experience with my college girlfriend and continue my marriage) and other psychodynamic themes. In the midst of all this clinical thinking a recent conversation with my wife came to mind. I told my wife (on the occasion of my 82nd birthday) that I hoped the next major event in my life would be my death. Somewhat familiar with such provocations, she asked me to explain. I told her that other major events—her death or that of one of our children or grandchildren would be catastrophic for me and with my career in its final stages—death as the next major life event seemed reasonable, even desirable. We talked on about this, and she seemed reassured that the idea made some sense and that I was not depressed.

The intrusion of this personal conversation into my mind while with the patient seemed at once of obvious importance in my efforts to understand the patient. At the time of his 80th birthday his wife went on a fun trip and he became preoccupied with re-establishing a youthful romantic relationship. Life is not nearly over; death is not the next major event; there is no need for depression; indeed, start anew. The problem, however, was that he could not pull it off. He could not risk losing his wife nor would his old girlfriend erase the inevitability of what was to come. Perched on the edge of existential despair, he searched for a solution that would not come.

These two examples—so different in their essential processes—are the types of experiences that make the work of psychotherapists so utterly fascinating.

October 2007

41

HEROIC ASPIRATIONS AND THE PSYCHOTHERAPIST

Some years ago a Sunday network television program presented during prime time the remarkable story of a brain surgeon. The program emphasized how often the impossible "cases" were referred to him, how delicate was his craft, and how well he continued to practice despite his own cancer. I watched riveted to the television set, and felt myself drawn deeply into this surgeon's life and work. For me he was a modern American hero.

At times in the intervening years I have wondered if the life and work of a psychotherapist could ever be presented in ways that accurately reflected the occasionally life-saving, perhaps even heroic, aspects of psychotherapy. Brain surgery is relatively easy to present in such terms; the surgeon is the ultimate hero, in some final way alone in the operating room doing battle with the evil forces of bursted blood vessels or cells gone wild.

In contrast how pale the work of the psychotherapist seems. He or she deals with feelings, words, defenses, stories, organizing themes, and encourages others to enter dark inner alleys, to learn to be in touch with distressing thoughts and feelings, to like oneself more than before, and to be able to stand up better for oneself. However much such treatment may help others to turn their lives around and, in some instances, actually save lives, it does not have the dramatic, moment-to-moment intensity of brain surgery. It is, after all, only conversation.

A 53 year old man is seen in consultation. He talks about his wife, her obesity and depression, and asks the clinician to see her. After these opening minutes of the interview the following exchange occurs.

Patient: "And that's it, Doctor, do you think you can help her?" (head down and with clear sadness)
Doctor: "You're very concerned about her and, well, you seem a little down yourself." (said with some tentativeness)
Patient: "Well. . . yes. My life is no picnic right now. Nothing seems to be going well." (with more open sadness)
Doctor: "It's more than your wife--it's your whole life."

The patient becomes silent and stares off with moistened eyes.

Doctor: "Hard to talk about." (softly)
Patient: (with a large sigh) "Our conflicts have driven both our kids away. Neither comes home, even for the holidays."
Doctor: "They seem lost from you."
Patient: "I'm all alone. Our friends have faded away . . . " (begins to cry)
Doctor: "It *really* sounds miserable."
Patient: "And then last week they promoted a younger guy rather than me . . . so it's clear. . . next they'll ask me about early retirement." (softly crying)
Doctor: "Everything seems over, gone—marriage, children, friends, job—how very sad." (with sadness)

By refusing to accept this man's opening statement about his wife as the major or only reason for the consultation and by responding empathically to the patient's feelings, the clinician makes contact with the pervasive depression and suicidality.

Patient: "And so I wonder, wonder about the future. What's out there for me?"
Doctor: "Is it all over or is there something out there?"
Patient: "Sometimes when I awake early in the morning and can't get back to sleep I think about the gun in my bedside table."
Doctor: "At those times it's tempting to go ahead and get it over with . . . "

Patient: "Yeah . . . it's very tempting. At those times everything seems hopeless."

Here the suicidal thoughts are brought into the open, paving the way for further exploration of the patient's risk to himself and, later in the interview, a discussion of the options available to prevent suicide.

All of this is just talk and seems a long way from the brain surgeon excising a brain tumor. In some ways it clearly is a long way, but in other regards there are similarities. The brain surgeon, for example, must be very delicate in getting to the tumor lest he do too much damage to surrounding normal brain tissue. The psychotherapist must also proceed with delicacy for if he or she is too bold the patient may retreat from disclosing the depth of his despair.

The brain surgeon must monitor the signs that suggest the surgery is compromising some vital function. The psychotherapist must also monitor signs that the exploration is moving too fast or too deep and the patient's psychological functioning is becoming compromised.

Both the brain surgeon and the psychotherapist move toward processes that cause death. Both risk losing the patient and in that loss possibly losing a part of their selves. There are studies demonstrating that such losses are experienced by many professionals at a deeply personal level.

Psychotherapists tend to discount the heroic aspects of their work, perhaps, in part, because as students we were taught that heroic aspirations were evidence of immaturity. This was before Ernest Becker wrote so cogently about the ubiquitous need to experience oneself as heroic (1). He described culture as a symbolic action system—a structure of statuses and roles, customs and rules—all designed to serve as guidelines for heroic behaviors. Man's tragic destiny is that he must justify himself as valuable, and, in the effort, he strives for heroism. The striving, however, is rarely acknowledged; indeed, Becker declares that the main self-analytic problem of life is to become conscious of what one is doing to earn his or her feeling of heroism. The absence of such awareness can lead to a blind drivenness that burns people up.

Thus, Becker does not believe that heroic aspirations reflect undue narcissism; rather they are a central part of normal psychological functioning springing from unconscious fears of both death and meaninglessness. McAdams, in his studies of narrative identity, suggests that heroic aspirations—the quest for symbolic immortality—are what fuels the engines of generativity, a prominent marker of adult maturity (2).

There are other reasons why psychotherapists discount a heroic component to their work. One is privacy. There are no assistants, anesthesiologists, or scrub nurses in the psychotherapist's office who might acknowledge the courage and skill required for a particular exploration. There is also confidentiality—the patient's right to be safe from possible exploitation. All of this and more combine to hide the fact that a skillful exploration of a dark and frightening passage in the life of another person does require highly developed skills, entails considerable risk, and may at times contain elements of the heroic. Unlikely, however, to be on primetime Sunday television.

References

1. Becker, E. (1973). *The Denial of Death*, New York: The Free Press.
2. McAdams, D.P. (1988). *Power, Intimacy, and the Life Story*, New York: The Guilford Press.

May 2005